Birds of the Dakotas

Field Guide

by Stan Tekiela

ADVENTURE PUBLICATIONS, INC.
CAMBRIDGE, MINNESOTA

TO MY WIFE KATHERINE AND DAUGHTER ABIGAIL
WITH ALL MY LOVE

ACKNOWLEDGMENTS:

Special thanks to Anthony Hertzel for range maps, and Dr. Dan Tallman, Editor, *South Dakota Bird Notes*, Northern State University, and Corey D. Ellingson, Compiler, *North Dakota Prairie Wings*, for reviewing them. Edited by Sandy Livoti.

Book design and illustrations by Jonathan Norberg

Photo credits by photographer and page number:

Cover photo: Male Baltimore Oriole by Stan Tekiela
Dominique Braud: 274 (adult) **Brian M. Collins:** 134, 180, 246 **Cornell Laboratory of Ornithology**: 66, 68 (female), 70 (perching) **Dudley Edmondson**: 10 (both), 12, 16 (breeding), 20, 22 (soaring), 52 (all), 74, 76, 82, 92 (both), 114 (adult), 118, 128 (in flight), 132, 140 (both), 142 (yellow-shafted male), 146, 148, 168 (soaring light morph), 170 (both), 174 (soaring juvenile), 176, 198 (male), 206, 216 (male), 218 (perching, soaring), 220, 222 (breeding), 224 (winter, displaying), 230, 262 (in flight), 264 (breeding), 272 (swimming), 276 (male, winter male), 278, 282 (male), 290, 294 **Don Enger**: 50 (rushing, weed dance) **Kevin T. Karlson**: 40, 42 (breeding), 152 (both) **Bruce Leventhal**: 268 **Bill Marchel**: 2, 28 (male), 34, 38, 68 (male), 80, 104 (white-striped), 110, 116, 138, 154, 160, 164, 186 (female), 198 (female), 236, 238 (both), 242, 248, 254, 270 (in flight) **Steve and Dave Maslowski**: 6 (male), 26, 54, 102, 108, 122 (female), 190, 204, 256, 258 (male), 274 (chick-feeding adult), 280, 286, 296 **Steve Mortensen**: 8, 28 (female), 36 (both), 44, 56, 58, 60 (both), 90 (both), 94, 162, 202, 240, 276 (female) **Warren Nelson**: 70 (soaring), 142 (yellow-shafted female), 282 (female) **John Pennoyer**: 46, 78, 124, 244, 252 (male) **Brian E. Small**: 16 (winter), 30 (breeding and non-breeding males), 32 (breeding male, female), 42 (winter), 50 (breeding), 62 (both), 84, 86, 96 (female), 98 (winter male), 100 (female), 120 (winter), 126 (female), 142 (red-shafted male and female), 150 (breeding), 156, 166, 178 (male), 210, 214 (male), 222 (winter), 250, 252 (yellow male), 260 (winter), 264 (winter, juvenile), 288 (all), 292 **Stan Tekiela**: 4 (both), 14, 18, 24 (both), 48, 64 (both), 72 (both), 88, 96 (breeding male), 98 (breeding male, female), 104 (tan-striped), 106 (both), 112, 114 (1 year old), 120 (breeding), 122 (juvenile), 128 (perching), 130, 136, 144, 158 (both), 172, 174 (perching, soaring), 178 (female), 182, 184, 186 (male), 188, 192, 194, 196, 200, 208, 212 (gray morph), 214 (female), 216 (female), 218 (juvenile), 228, 232, 234, 260 (breeding), 262 (perching), 266 (all), 270 (swimming), 272 (in flight, juvenile), 284 (both) **Brian K. Wheeler**: 22 (perching), 168 (perching light and dark morphs, soaring dark morph, intermediate morph), 174 (juvenile), 226 (all) **Jim Zipp**: 32 (winter male), 114 (Bohemian), 212 (red morph)

To the best of the publisher's knowledge, all photographs were of live birds.

Copyright 2003 by Stan Tekiela
Published by Adventure Publications, Inc.
820 Cleveland Street South
Cambridge, MN 55008
1-800-678-7006
www.adventurepublications.net
All rights reserved
Printed in China
ISBN-13: 978-1-59193-016-7
ISBN-10: 1-59193-016-2

TABLE OF CONTENTS

Introduction

Why Watch Birds in the Dakotas? iv

Observe with a Strategy; Tips for Identifying Birds............................. v

Bird Basics viii

Bird Color Variables viii

Bird Nests x

Who Builds the Nest?... xiii

Fledging xiii

Why Birds Migrate xiii

How Do Birds Migrate? xv

How to Use This Guide xvi

Range Maps xvi

Sample Page 1

The Birds

Black 3

Black and White 27

Blue 55

Brown.. 71

Gray 191

Green 239

Orange 247

Red 253

White 263

Yellow 277

Helpful Resources 298

Check List/Index 300

About the Author... 303

WHY WATCH BIRDS IN THE DAKOTAS?

Millions of people have discovered bird feeding. It's a simple and enjoyable way to bring the beauty of birds closer to your home. Watching birds at your feeder often leads to a lifetime pursuit of bird identification. The *Birds of the Dakotas Field Guide* is for those who want to identify the common birds of North Dakota and South Dakota.

There are over 800 species of birds found in North America. In North and South Dakota there has been over 400 different kinds of birds recorded in both states throughout the years. That is an impressive number of species for the two states! These bird sightings were diligently recorded by hundreds of bird watchers and became part of the official state records. From these valuable records, I have chosen 125 of the most common birds of the Dakotas to include in this field guide.

Bird watching, often called birding, is the largest spectator sport in America. Its outstanding popularity in the Dakotas is due, in part, to an unusually rich and abundant birdlife. Why are there so many birds? One reason is open space. North Dakota is over 70,700 square miles (183,800 sq. km) and is the eighteenth largest state. South Dakota is even larger, covering more than 77,100 square miles (200,400 sq. km), and is the seventeenth largest state. Combined, these states make up a large portion of the North Central region and provide the majority of nesting habitats for a large number of birds, especially waterfowl in this area of the U.S.

Vast open spaces in the Dakotas are not the only reason there is such an abundance of birds. It's also the diversity of habitat. The Dakotas can be broken into two distinct regions, each of which supports a different group of birds.

The highest and driest part of the Dakotas is in the western half. Called the Great Plains, this region has major features that are quite unlike its wide open plains. The Black Hills and Badlands are highly unique jewels and wonderful places to see birds such as Western Tanagers and Lazuli Buntings. The rest of the region is a relatively flat, open space that was once short grass prairie, but is now mostly agricultural. Horned Larks, Lark Buntings, Western Kingbirds and many other open country birds can be found here.

The eastern half of the Dakotas is exemplified by the wide, flat, former lake bottom known as Glacial Lake Agassiz. This region, with its many temporary ponds and lakes, is much wetter than its western counterpart. These habitats provide very important breeding grounds for waterfowl such as Gadwalls and Mallards.

Not only do the Dakotas have varying habitats, there are variations in the weather. Since the two states extend over 450 miles (725 km) from north to south, the weather ranges greatly. While summers can be extremely hot and steamy, the high winds and driving snows of winter are legendary.

No matter where you are in the Dakotas there are birds to watch in every season. Whether witnessing a migration of millions of waterfowl in autumn or welcoming back shorebirds in spring, there is variety and excitement in birding as each season turns to the next.

OBSERVE WITH A STRATEGY; TIPS FOR IDENTIFYING BIRDS

Identifying birds isn't as difficult as you might think. By simply following a few basic strategies, you can increase your chances of successfully identifying most birds you see! One of the first and easiest things to do when you see a new bird is to note its color. (Also, since this book is organized by color, you will go right to that color section to find it.)

Next, note the size of the bird. A strategy to quickly estimate size is to select a small-, medium- and large-sized bird to use for reference. For example, most people are familiar with robins. A robin, measured from tip of the bill to tip of the tail, is 10 inches (25 cm) long. Using the robin as an example of a medium-sized bird, select two other birds, one smaller and one larger. Many people use a House Sparrow, at about 6 inches (15 cm), and an American Crow, about 18 inches (45 cm). When you see a bird that you don't know, you can quickly ask yourself, "Is it smaller than a robin, but larger than a sparrow?" When you look in your field guide to help identify your bird, you'll know it's roughly between 6 and 10 inches (15 to 25 cm) long. This will help to narrow your choices.

Next, note the size, shape and color of the bill. Is it long, short, thick, thin, pointed, blunt, curved or straight? Seed-eating birds, such as Northern Cardinals, have bills that are thick and strong enough to crack even the toughest seeds. Birds that sip nectar, such as Ruby-throated Hummingbirds, need long thin bills to reach deep into flowers. Hawks and owls tear their prey with very sharp, curving bills. Sometimes, just noting the bill shape can help you decide if the bird is a woodpecker, finch, grosbeak, blackbird or bird of prey.

Next, take a look around and note the habitat in which you see the bird. Is it wading in a marsh? Walking along a riverbank? Soaring in the sky? Is it perched high in the trees or hopping along the forest floor? Because of their preferences in diet and habitat, you'll usually see robins hopping on the ground, but not often eating the seeds at your feeder. Or you'll see a Rose-breasted Grosbeak sitting on a branch of a tree, but not climbing down the tree trunk headfirst the way a nuthatch does.

Noticing what a bird is eating will give you another clue to help you identify that bird. Feeding is a big part of any bird's life. Fully one-third of all bird activity revolves around searching for and catching food, or actually eating. While birds don't always follow all the rules of what we think they eat, you can make some general assumptions. Northern Flickers, for instance, feed upon ants and other insects, so you wouldn't expect to see them visiting a backyard feeder. Some birds, such as Barn Swallows and Cliff Swallows, feed upon flying insects, and spend hours swooping and diving to catch a meal.

Sometimes you can identify a bird by the way it perches. Body posture can help you differentiate between an American Crow and a Red-tailed Hawk. American Crows lean forward over their feet on a branch, while hawks perch in a vertical position. Look for this the next time you see a large unidentified bird in a tree.

Birds in flight are often difficult to identify, but noting the size and shape of the wing will help. A bird's wing size is in direct proportion to its body size, weight and type of flying. The shape of the wing determines if the bird flies fast and with precision, or slowly and less precisely. Birds such as House Finches, which flit around in thick tangles of branches, have short round wings. Birds that soar on warm updrafts of air, such as Turkey Vultures, have long broad wings. Barn Swallows have short pointed wings that slice through air, propelling their swift and accurate flight.

Some birds have unique flight patterns that aid in identification. American Goldfinches fly in a distinctive up-and-down pattern that makes it look as if they are riding a roller coaster.

While it's not easy to make these observations in the short time you often have to watch a "mystery bird," practicing these methods of identification will greatly expand your skills in birding. Also, seek the guidance of a more experienced birder who will help you improve your skills and answer questions on the spot.

BIRD BASICS

It's easier to identify birds and communicate about them if you know the names of the different parts of a bird. For instance, it's more effective to use the word "crest" to indicate the set of extra long feathers on top of a Northern Cardinal's head than to try to describe it.

The following illustration points out the basic parts of a bird. Because it is a composite of many birds, it shouldn't be confused with any actual bird.

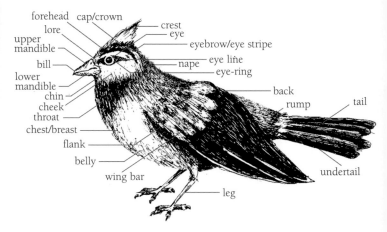

forehead cap/crown
lore
upper mandible
bill
lower mandible
chin
cheek
throat
chest/breast
flank
belly
wing bar

crest
eye
eyebrow/eye stripe
nape eye line
eye-ring
back
rump
tail
undertail
leg

BIRD COLOR VARIABLES

No other animal has a color pallet like a bird's. Brilliant blues, lemon yellows, showy reds and iridescent greens are common-place within the bird world. In general, the male birds are more colorful than their female counterparts. This is probably to help the male attract a mate, essentially saying, "Hey, look at me!" It also calls attention to the male's overall health. The better the condition of his feathers, the better his food source and territory, and therefore the better his potential for a mate.

Female birds that don't look like their male counterparts (such species are called sexually dimorphic, meaning "two forms") are often a nondescript color, as seen with Rose-breasted Grosbeaks. These muted tones help to hide the females during weeks of motionless incubation, and draw less attention to them when they are out feeding or taking a break from the rigors of raising their young.

In some species, such as the Bald Eagle, Blue Jay and Downy Woodpecker, the male birds look nearly identical to the females. In the case of the woodpeckers, the sexes are only differentiated by a single red or sometimes yellow mark. Depending on the species, the mark may be on top of the head, face, nape of the neck or just behind the bill.

During the first year, juvenile birds often look like the mothers. Since brightly colored feathers are used mainly for attracting a mate, young non-breeding males don't have a need for colorful plumage. It is not until the first spring molt (or several years later, depending on the species) that young males obtain their breeding colors.

Both breeding and winter plumages are the result of molting. Molting is the process of dropping old worn feathers and replacing them with new ones. All birds molt, typically twice a year, with the spring molt usually occurring in late winter. During this time, most birds produce their breeding plumage (brighter colors for attracting mates), which lasts throughout the summer.

Winter plumage is the result of the late summer molt, which serves a couple of important functions. First, it adds feathers for warmth in the coming winter. Second, in some species it produces feathers that tend to be drab in color, which helps to camouflage the birds and hide them from predators. The winter plumage of the male American Goldfinch, for example, is an olive brown, unlike its obvious canary yellow color in summer. Luckily for us, some birds, such as the male Northern Cardinal, retain their bright summer colors all year long.

BIRD NESTS

Bird nests are truly an amazing feat of engineering. Imagine building your home strong enough to weather a storm, large enough to hold your entire family, insulated enough to shelter them from cold and heat, and waterproof enough to keep out rain. Now, build it without any blueprints or directions, and without the use of your hands or feet! Birds do!

Before building a nest, an appropriate site must be selected. In some species, such as House Wrens, the male picks out several potential sites and assembles several small twigs in each. This discourages other birds from using nearby nest cavities. These "extra" nests are occasionally called dummy nests. The female is then taken around and shown all the choices. She chooses her favorite and finishes constructing the nest. In some other species of birds–Baltimore Orioles, for example–it is the female who chooses the site and builds the nest with the male offering only an occasional suggestion. Each species has its own nest-building routine, which is strictly followed.

Nesting material usually consists of natural elements found in the immediate area. Most nests consist of plant fibers (such as bark peeled from grapevines), sticks, mud, dried grass, feathers, fur, or soft fuzzy tufts from thistle. Some birds, including Ruby-throated Hummingbirds, use spider webs to glue nest materials together. Nesting material is limited to what a bird can hold or carry. Because of this, a bird must make many trips afield to gather enough materials to complete its nest. Most nests take at least four days or more, and hundreds, if not thousands, of trips to build.

As you'll see in the following illustrations, birds build a wide variety of nest types.

ground nest   platform nest   cup nest   pendulous nest

The simple **ground nest** is scraped out of the earth. A shallow depression that usually contains no nesting material, it is made by birds such as the Killdeer and Horned Lark.

Another kind of nest, the **platform nest**, represents a more complex type of nest building. Constructed of small twigs and branches, the platform nest is a simple arrangement of sticks which forms a platform and features a small depression to nestle the eggs.

Some platform nests, such as those of the Canada Goose, are constructed on the ground and are made with mud and grass. Platform nests can also be on cliffs, bridges, balconies or even in flowerpots. This kind of nest gives space to adventurous young-sters and functions as a landing platform for the parents. Many waterfowl construct platform nests on the ground, usually near water or actually in the water. These floating platform nests vary with the water level, thus preventing nests with eggs from being flooded. Platform nests, constructed by such birds as Mourning Doves and herons, are not anchored to the tree and may tumble from the branches during high winds and storms.

The **cup nest** is a modified platform nest, used by three-quarters of all songbirds. Constructed from the outside in, a supporting platform is constructed first. This platform is attached firmly to a tree, shrub, rock ledge or the ground. Next, the sides are con-structed of grasses, small twigs, bark or leaves, which are woven together and often glued with mud for additional strength. The inner cup, lined with feathers, animal fur, soft plant material or animal hair, is constructed last. The mother bird uses her chest to cast the final contours of the inner nest.

The **pendulous nest** is an unusual nest, looking more like a sock hanging from a branch than a nest. Inaccessible to most predators, these nests are attached to the ends of the smallest branches of a tree, and often wave wildly in the breeze. Woven very tightly of plant fibers, they are strong and watertight, taking up to a week to build. More commonly used by tropical birds, this complicated nest type has also been mastered by orioles and kinglets. A small opening on the top or side allows the parents access to the grass-lined interior. (It must be one heck of a ride to be inside one of these nests during a windy spring thunderstorm!)

One of the most clever of all nest types is known as the **no nest** or daycare nest. Parasitic birds, such as Brown-headed Cowbirds, build no nests at all! The egg-laden female expertly searches out other birds' nests and sneaks in to lay one of her own eggs while the host mother is not looking, thereby leaving the host mother to raise an adopted youngster. The mother cowbird wastes no energy building a nest only to have it raided by a predator. By using several nests of other birds, she spreads out her progeny so at least one of her offspring will live to maturity.

Another type of nest, the **cavity nest**, is used by many birds, including woodpeckers and Eastern Bluebirds. The cavity nest is usually excavated in a tree branch or trunk and offers shelter from storms, sun, predators and cold. A relatively small entrance hole in a tree leads to an inner chamber up to 10 inches (25 cm) below. Usually constructed by woodpeckers, the cavity nest is typically used only once by its builder, but subsequently can be used for many years by birds such as Wood Ducks, Tree Swallows and bluebirds, which do not have the capability of excavating one for themselves. Kingfishers, on the other hand, excavate a tunnel up to 4 feet (1 m) long, which connects the entrance in a riverbank to the nest chamber. These cavity nests are often sparsely lined because they are already well insulated.

Some birds, including some swallows, take nest building one step further. They use a collection of small balls of mud to construct an adobe-style home. Constructed beneath the eaves of houses, under bridges or inside chimneys, some of these nests look like simple cup nests. Others are completely enclosed, with small tunnel-like openings that lead into a safe nesting chamber for the baby birds.

WHO BUILDS THE NEST?

In general, the female bird builds the nest. She gathers nesting materials and constructs a nest, with an occasional visit from her mate to check on the progress. In some species, both parents contribute equally to the construction of a nest. A male bird might forage for precisely the right sticks, grass or mud, but it's often the female that forms or puts together the nest. She uses her body to form the egg chamber. Rarely does the male build a nest by himself.

FLEDGING

Fledging is the interval between hatching and flight or leaving the nest. Some birds leave the nest within hours of hatching (precocial), but it might be weeks before they are able to fly. This is common with waterfowl and shorebirds. Until they start to fly, they are called fledglings. Birds that are still in the nest are called nestlings. Other baby birds are born naked and blind, and remain in the nest for several weeks (altricial).

WHY BIRDS MIGRATE

Why do birds migrate? The short answer is simple–food. Birds migrate to areas with high concentrations of food, as it is easier to breed where food is than where it is not. A typical migrating bird–the Rose-breasted Grosbeak, for instance–migrates from the tropics of Central and South America to nest in the forests of North America, taking advantage of billions of newly hatched insects to feed its young. This trip is called **complete migration**.

Some birds of prey return from their complete migration to northern regions that are overflowing with small rodents, such as mice and voles, that have continued to breed in winter.

Complete migrators have a set time and pattern of migration. Each year at nearly the same time, they take off and head for a specific wintering ground. Complete migrators may travel great distances, sometimes as much as 15,000 miles (24,150 km) or more in a year. But complete migration doesn't necessarily imply flying from the cold, frozen northland to a tropical destination. The Dark-eyed Junco, for example, is a complete migrator that flies from the far reaches of Canada to spend the winter right here in the Dakotas.

There are many interesting aspects to complete migrators. In the spring, males usually migrate several weeks before the females, arriving early to scope out possibilities for nesting sites and food sources, and to begin to defend territories. The females arrive several weeks later. In the autumn, in many species, the females and their young leave early, often up to four weeks before the adult males.

All migrators are not the same type. There are **partial migrators**, such as American Goldfinches, that usually wait until the food supply dwindles before flying south. Unlike complete migrators, the partial migrators move only far enough south, or sometimes east and west, to find abundant food. In some years it might be only a few hundred miles, while in other years it might be nearly a thousand. This kind of migration, dependent on the weather and available food, is sometimes called **seasonal movement**.

Unlike the predictable ebbing and flowing behavior of complete migrators or partial migrators, **irruptive migrators** can move every third to fifth year or, in some cases, in consecutive years. These migrations are triggered when times are really tough and food is scarce. Red-breasted Nuthatches are a good example of irruptive migrators, because they leave their normal northern range in search of food or in response to overpopulation.

How Do Birds Migrate?

One of the many secrets of migration is fat. While we humans are fighting the battle of the bulge, birds intentionally gorge themselves to put on as much fat as possible while still being able to fly. Fat provides the greatest amount of energy per unit of weight, and in the same way that your car needs gas, birds are propelled by fat and stalled without it.

During long migratory flights, fat deposits are used up quickly, and birds need to stop to "refuel." This is when backyard bird feeding stations and undeveloped, natural spaces around our towns and cities are especially important. Some birds require up to two to three days of constant feeding to build up their fat reserves before continuing their seasonal trip.

Some birds, such as most eagles, hawks, falcons and vultures, migrate during the day. Larger birds can hold more body fat, go longer without eating and take longer to migrate. These birds glide on rising columns of warm air, called thermals, which hold them aloft while they slowly make their way north or south. They generally rest during nights and hunt early in the morning before the sun has a chance to warm up the land and create good soaring conditions. Birds migrating during the day use a combination of landforms, rivers, and the rising and setting sun to guide them in the right direction.

Most other birds migrate during the night. Studies show that some birds which migrate at night use the stars to navigate. Others use the setting sun, while still others, such as doves, use the earth's magnetic fields to guide them north or south. While flying at night might seem like a crazy idea, nocturnal migration is safer for several reasons. First, there are fewer nighttime predators for migrating birds. Second, traveling at night allows time during the day to find food in unfamiliar surroundings. Finally, nighttime wind patterns tend to be flat, or laminar. These flat winds don't have the turbulence associated with the daytime winds and can actually help carry smaller birds by pushing them along.

HOW TO USE THIS GUIDE

To help you quickly and easily identify birds, this book is organized by color. Simply note the color of the bird and turn to that section. Refer to the first page for the color key. The male Rose-breasted Grosbeak, for example, is black-and-white with a red patch on its chest. Because the bird is mostly black and white, it will be found in the black and white section. Each color section is also arranged by size, generally with the smaller birds first. Sections may also incorporate the average size in a range, which, in some cases, reflects size differences between male and female birds. Flip through the pages in that color section to find the bird. If you already know the name of the bird, check the index for the page number. In some species, the male and female are remarkably different in color. In these cases, the opposite sex is shown in a smaller inset photograph with a page reference. These birds, therefore, will be found in two different color sections.

In the description section you will find a variety of information about the bird. On the next page is a sample of the information included in the book.

RANGE MAPS

Range maps are included for each bird. Colored areas indicate where in the Dakotas a particular bird is most likely to be found. The colors represent the presence of a species during a specific season, not the density or amount of birds in the area. Green is used for summer, blue for winter, red for year-round and yellow for areas where the bird is seen during migration. While every effort has been made to accurately depict these ranges, they are only general guidelines. Ranges actually change on an ongoing basis due to a variety of factors. Changes in weather, species abundance, landscape and vital resources such as the availability of food and water can affect local populations, migration and movements, causing birds to be found in areas that are atypical for the species.

Colored areas simply mean bird sightings for that species have been frequent in those areas and less frequent in the others. Please use the maps as intended–as general guides only.

COMMON NAME
Scientific name

YEAR-ROUND
MIGRATION
SUMMER
WINTER

Size: measures head to tail, may include wingspan

Male: a brief description of the male bird, and may include breeding, winter or other plumages

Female: a brief description of the female bird, which is sometimes not the same as the male

Juvenile: a brief description of the juvenile bird, which often looks like the female

Nest: the kind of nest this bird builds to raise its young; who builds the nest; how many broods per year

Eggs: how many eggs you might expect to see in a nest; color and marking

Incubation: the average time parents spend incubating the eggs; who does the incubation

Fledging: the average time young spend in the nest after hatching but before they leave the nest; who does the most "childcare" and feeding

Migration: complete (consistent, seasonal), partial migrator (seasonal, destination varies), irruptive (unpredictable, depends on the food supply), non-migrator; additional comments

Food: what the bird eats most of the time (e.g., seeds, insects, fruit, nectar, small mammals, fish); if it typically comes to a bird feeding station

Compare: notes about other birds that look similar, and the pages on which they can be found

Stan's Notes: Interesting gee-whiz natural history information. This could be something to look or listen for, or something to help positively identify the bird. Also includes remarkable features.

1

female pg. 119

male

BROWN-HEADED COWBIRD
Molothrus ater

Size: 7½" (19 cm)

Male: A glossy black bird, reminiscent of a Red-winged Blackbird. Chocolate brown head with a pointed, sharp gray bill.

Female: dull brown bird with bill similar to male

Juvenile: similar to female, only dull gray color and a streaked chest

Nest: no nest; lays eggs in nests of other birds

Eggs: 5-7; white with brown markings

Incubation: 10-13 days; host bird incubates eggs

Fledging: 10-11 days; host birds feed young

Migration: complete, to southern states

Food: insects, seeds; will come to seed feeders

Compare: The male Red-winged Blackbird (pg. 9) is slightly larger, with red and yellow patches on upper wings. Common Grackle (pg. 15) has a long tail and lacks the brown head. European Starling (pg. 5) has a shorter tail.

Stan's Notes: A member of the blackbird family. Of approximately 750 species of parasitic birds worldwide, this is the only parasitic bird in the Dakotas, laying eggs in host birds' nests, leaving others to raise its young. Cowbirds are known to have laid eggs in nests of over 200 species of birds. Some birds reject cowbird eggs, but most incubate them and raise the young, even to the exclusion of their own. Look for warblers and other birds feeding young birds twice their own size. At one time cowbirds followed bison to feed on insects attracted to the animals.

3

winter

breeding

EUROPEAN STARLING
Sturnus vulgaris

Size:	7½" (19 cm)
Male:	Gray-to-black bird with white speckles in fall and winter. Shiny purple black during spring and summer. Long, pointed yellow bill in spring turns gray in fall. Short tail.
Female:	same as male
Juvenile:	similar to adult, gray brown in color with a streaked chest
Nest:	cavity; male and female line the cavity; 2 broods per year
Eggs:	4-6; bluish with brown markings
Incubation:	12-14 days; female and male incubate
Fledging:	18-20 days; female and male feed young
Migration:	non-migrator to partial migrator; some will move to southern states
Food:	insects, seeds, fruit; comes to seed and suet feeders
Compare:	Looks similar to Common Grackle (pg. 15), but lacks its long tail.

Stan's Notes: A great songster, this bird can also mimic sounds. Often displaces woodpeckers, chickadees and other cavity-nesting birds. Can be very aggressive and destroy eggs or young of other birds. The bill changes color with the seasons: yellow in spring and gray in autumn. Jaws are designed to be the most powerful when opening, as they pry open crevices to locate hidden insects. Gathers in the hundreds in autumn. Not a native bird, it was introduced to New York City in 1890-91 from Europe.

female pg. 127

male

SPOTTED TOWHEE
Pipilo maculatus

MIGRATION
SUMMER

Size: 8½" (22 cm)

Male: A mostly black bird with dirty red-brown sides and white belly. Multiple white spots on wings and sides. Long black tail with a white tip. Rich red eyes.

Female: very similar to male, with a brown head

Juvenile: brown with a heavily streaked chest

Nest: cup; female builds; 1-2 broods per year

Eggs: 3-5; white with brown markings

Incubation: 12-14 days; female and male incubate

Fledging: 10-12 days; female and male feed young

Migration: partial migrator

Food: seeds, fruit, insects

Compare: Smaller than American Robin (pg. 217). Male Rose-breasted Grosbeak (pg. 35) has a rosy patch in center of chest.

Stan's Notes: Summer visitor in western and southern parts of the Dakotas and seen during migration. Found in a variety of habitats from thick brush and forest edges to suburban backyards. Often can be heard noisily scratching through dead leaves on the ground as it searches for food. While over 70 percent of its diet is plant material, it eats more insects in spring and summer. Well known to retreat from danger, walking away rather than taking to flight. Cup nest is nearly always on the ground underneath bushes, away from where male perches to sing. Song and plumage vary geographically and are not well studied or understood.

female pg. 124

male

RED-WINGED BLACKBIRD
Agelaius phoeniceus

**YEAR-ROUND
SUMMER**

Size:	8½" (22 cm)
Male:	Jet black bird with red and yellow shoulder patches on upper wings. Pointed black bill.
Female:	heavily streaked brown bird with a pointed brown bill and white eyebrows
Juvenile:	same as female
Nest:	cup; female builds; 2-3 broods per year
Eggs:	3-4; bluish green with brown markings
Incubation:	10-12 days; female incubates
Fledging:	11-14 days; female and male feed young
Migration:	complete to partial migrator, to southern states, Mexico and Central America; moves around to find food
Food:	seeds, insects; will come to seed feeders
Compare:	Slightly larger than the male Brown-headed Cowbird (pg. 3), but is less iridescent and lacks Cowbird's brown head. Differs from all blackbirds due to the red and yellow patches on its wings (epaulets).

Stan's Notes: One of the most widespread and numerous birds in the Dakotas. It is a sure sign of spring when Red-winged Blackbirds return to the marshes. Flocks of up to 100,000 birds have been reported. Males return before the females and defend territories by singing from tops of surrounding vegetation. Males repeat call from the tops of cattails while showing off their red and yellow wing bars (epaulets). Females choose mate and usually will nest over shallow water in thick stands of cattails. Red-wingeds feed mostly on seeds in fall and spring, switching to insects during summer.

in flight

BLACK TERN
Chlidonias niger

Size: 9¾" (24.5 cm)

Male: Breeding plumage (March to September) head, neck and body are black. Back, wings and tail are gray. Dark eyes, bill and legs. Winter is overall gray with a nearly white head and white undertail. Pale yellow legs.

Female: same as male

Juvenile: similar to winter adult, back is more brown than gray

Nest: floating platform; male and female build; 1-2 broods per year

Eggs: 2-4; green with brown markings

Incubation: 21-22 days; female and male incubate

Fledging: 21-28 days; male and female feed young

Migration: complete, to South America

Food: insects, small fish, aquatic insects

Compare: The only tern with a black head and body.

Stan's Notes: Common breeding bird in prairie potholes, nesting in small colonies. The nest is often just a floating mat of vegetation. Often will use an old grebe nest. Young females begin to breed at 2 years of age. Aggressively defends nest site and young. Will dive at intruders and predators. Has a unique buoyant flight pattern, with erratic swoops. Unlike other tern species, rarely plunges into water after prey. Hunts for insects on surfaces of ponds and marshes and picks insects out of the air. Occasionally follows plows to pick off insects disturbed in fields. Gives a sharp "keff" call while in flight. Migrates in large flocks.

female pg. 133

male

YELLOW-HEADED BLACKBIRD
Xanthocephalus xanthocephalus

Size: 9-11" (22.5-28 cm)

Male: Large black bird with a lemon yellow head, chest and nape of neck. Black mask and a gray bill. White wing patches.

Female: similar to male, only slightly smaller with a brown body, dull yellow head and chest

Juvenile: similar to female

Nest: cup; female builds; 2 broods per year

Eggs: 3-5; greenish white with brown markings

Incubation: 11-13 days; female incubates

Fledging: 9-12 days; female feeds young

Migration: complete, to southern states and Mexico

Food: insects, seeds

Compare: Larger than the male Red-winged Blackbird (pg. 9), which has red and yellow patches on its wings. Male Yellow-headed Blackbird is the only large black bird with a bright yellow head.

Stan's Notes: Usually heard before seen, Yellow-headed Blackbird has a low, hoarse, raspy or metallic call. Nests in deep water marshes unlike its cousin, the Red-winged Blackbird, which prefers shallow water. The male gives an impressive mating display, flying with head drooped and feet and tail pointing down while steadily beating its wings. The female incubates alone and feeds between three to five young. Young keep low and out of sight for up to three weeks before starting to fly. Migrates in flocks of up to 200 with other blackbirds. Flocks made up mainly of males return first in late March and early April; females return later. Most colonies consist of 20 to 100 nests.

COMMON GRACKLE
Quiscalus quiscula

YEAR-ROUND
SUMMER

Size: 11-13" (28-33 cm)

Male: Large black bird with iridescent blue black head, purple brown body, long black tail, long thin bill and bright golden eyes.

Female: similar to male, only duller and smaller

Juvenile: similar to female

Nest: cup; female builds; 2 broods per year

Eggs: 4-5; greenish white with brown markings

Incubation: 13-14 days; female incubates

Fledging: 16-20 days; female and male feed young

Migration: complete to partial, to southern states; will move around to find food

Food: fruit, seeds, insects; comes to seed feeders

Compare: European Starling (pg. 5) is much smaller with a speckled appearance, and yellow bill during the breeding season. The male Red-winged Blackbird (pg. 9) has red and yellow wing markings.

Stan's Notes: Usually nests in small colonies of up to 75 pairs, but travels with other blackbirds in large flocks. Is known to feed in farmers' fields. The name is derived from the Latin word *graculus*, meaning "to cough," for its loud raspy call. Male holds tail in a vertical keel-like position during flight. The flight pattern is almost always level, as opposed to an undulating up-and-down movement. Unlike most birds, it has larger muscles for opening the mouth (rather than for closing it) and prying crevices apart to locate hidden insects.

15

winter

breeding

EARED GREBE
Podiceps nigricollis

Size: 13" (33 cm)

Male: Breeding plumage (April to August) head, neck and back overall dark brown to black. Sides and chest are chestnut brown. Wispy yellow plumes feather out behind red eyes. Small black bill. Winter plumage chin and sides are dirty brown to black and white. Red eyes and a dark-tipped gray bill.

Female: same as male

Juvenile: similar to winter adult

Nest: floating platform; female and male build; 1-2 broods per year

Eggs: 3-5; light blue with brown markings

Incubation: 20-22 days; female and male incubate

Fledging: 20-40 days; male and female teach young what to eat

Migration: complete, to Pacific and Gulf coasts, Mexico

Food: fish, aquatic insects

Compare: Horned Grebe (pg. 261) is slightly larger, with a rufous neck during breeding season.

Stan's Notes: A grebe of pothole lakes and ponds, nesting in large colonies. Builds a platform nest in shallow water, made from reeds and grasses. Often constructs more than one nest. A few days after hatching, the young are fed small feathers. Feather eating pads the stomach and is thought to aid the digestion of fish and fish bones. Chick siblings are not the same size, since young hatch several days apart. Chicks ride on backs of parents. Often dives underwater to avoid danger, remaining submerged with just its bill above water.

SUMMER

AMERICAN COOT
Fulica americana

Size: 13-16" (33-40 cm)

Male: Slate gray to black all over, white bill with dark band near tip. Green legs and feet. A small white patch near the base of the tail. Prominent red eyes, with a small red patch above bill between eyes.

Female: same as male

Juvenile: much paler than adult, with a gray bill and same white rump patch

Nest: cup; female and male build; 1 brood per year

Eggs: 9-12; pinkish buff with brown markings

Incubation: 21-25 days; female and male incubate

Fledging: 49-52 days; female and male feed young

Migration: complete, to southern states, Mexico and Central America

Food: insects, aquatic plants

Compare: Smaller than most waterfowl, it is the only black water bird or duck-like bird with a white bill.

Stan's Notes: An excellent diver and swimmer, often seen in large flocks on open water. Not a duck, as it doesn't have webbed feet, but instead has large lobed toes. When taking off, scrambles across surface of water with wings flapping. Bobs head while swimming. Floating nests are anchored to vegetation. Huge flocks of up to 1,000 birds gather for fall migration. The unusual name is of unknown origin, but in Middle English, the word *coote* was used to describe various waterfowl–perhaps it stuck. Also called Mud Hen.

AMERICAN CROW
Corvus brachyrhynchos

YEAR-ROUND
SUMMER

Size: 18" (45 cm)

Male: All-black bird with black bill, legs and feet. Can have a purple sheen in direct sunlight.

Female: same as male

Juvenile: same as adult

Nest: platform; female builds; 1 brood per year

Eggs: 4-6; bluish to olive green, brown markings

Incubation: 18 days; female incubates

Fledging: 28-35 days; female and male feed young

Migration: non-migrator to partial migrator

Food: fruit, insects, mammals, fish, carrion; will come to seed and suet feeders

Compare: Black-billed Magpie (pg. 47) has a long tail and white belly. Similar to Common Raven (not shown), but has a smaller bill and lacks shaggy throat feathers. The Crow has a higher-pitched call than Raven's deep, low raspy call. Crow has a squared tail. Raven has a wedge-shaped tail, apparent in flight.

Stan's Notes: One of the most recognizable birds in the Dakotas. It will often reuse its nest every year if not taken over by a Great Horned Owl. Collects and stores bright, shiny objects in nest. Able to mimic other birds and human voices. One of the smartest of all birds and very social, often entertaining itself by provoking chases with other birds. Feeds on road kill but is rarely hit by cars. Can live up to 20 years. Unmated birds, known as helpers, help raise young. Large extended families roost together at night, dispersing during the day to hunt.

soaring

TURKEY VULTURE
Cathartes aura

SUMMER

Size: 26-32" (66-80 cm); up to 6-foot wingspan

Male: Large bird with obvious red head and legs. In flight, the wings appear two-toned: black leading edge with gray on the trailing edge and tip. The tips of wings end in finger-like projections. Long squared tail. Ivory bill.

Female: same as male

Juvenile: similar to adult, with gray-to-blackish head and bill

Nest: no nest, or minimal nest on cliff or in cave; 1 brood per year

Eggs: 2; white with brown markings

Incubation: 38-41 days; female and male incubate

Fledging: 66-88 days; female and male feed young

Migration: complete, to southern states, Mexico, and Central and South America

Food: carrion, just about any dead animal of any size; parents regurgitate for young

Compare: Smaller than the Bald Eagle (pg. 53), look for Vulture's two-toned wings. Flies holding wings in a slight V shape, unlike the Eagle's straight wing position.

Stan's Notes: The vulture's naked head is an adaptation to reduce risk of feather fouling (picking up diseases) from carcasses. Unlike hawks and eagles, it has weak feet more suited to walking than grasping. One of the few birds that has a developed sense of smell. Mostly mute, making only grunts and groans. Seen in trees with wings outstretched to catch sun.

drying

DOUBLE-CRESTED CORMORANT
Phalacrocorax auritus

SUMMER

Size: 33" (84 cm)

Male: Large all-black water bird with long snake-like neck. A long yellow orange bill with a hooked tip.

Female: same as male

Juvenile: lighter brown with a grayish-colored breast and neck

Nest: platform, in colony; male and female build; 1 brood per year

Eggs: 3-4; bluish white without markings

Incubation: 25-29 days; female and male incubate

Fledging: 37-42 days; male and female feed young

Migration: complete, to southern states, Mexico and Central America

Food: small fish, aquatic insects

Compare: Similar size as the Turkey Vulture (pg. 23), which also perches on branches with wings open to dry in sun, but Vulture has a naked red head. Twice the size of American Coot (pg. 19), which lacks the Cormorant's long neck and long pointed bill.

Stan's Notes: Often seen flying in large V formation. Often roosts in large groups in trees near water. Catches fish by swimming with wings held at its sides. To dry off it strikes an erect pose with wings outstretched, facing the sun. The name refers to its nearly invisible crests. "Cormorant" comes from the Latin *corvus*, meaning "crow," and *L. marinus*, meaning "pertaining to the sea," literally, "Sea Crow."

BLACK-AND-WHITE WARBLER
Mniotilta varia

Size: 5" (13 cm)

Male: Striped like a zebra, this small warbler has a distinctive black-and-white striped cap. White belly. Black chin and cheek patch.

Female: same as male, only duller and without the black chin and cheek patch

Juvenile: similar to female

Nest: cup; female builds; 1 brood per year

Eggs: 4-5; white with brown markings

Incubation: 10-11 days; female incubates

Fledging: 9-12 days; female and male feed young

Migration: complete, to Florida, Mexico, Central and South America

Food: insects

Compare: Look for Warbler to creep down tree trunks headfirst, like the Red-breasted and White-breasted Nuthatches (pp. 193 and 197).

Stan's Notes: The only warbler that moves headfirst down a tree trunk. Look for this common warbler searching for insect eggs in the bark of large trees. Song sounds like a slowly turning, squeaky wheel. Female will perform a distraction dance to draw predators away from the nest. Makes its nest on the ground, concealed under dead leaves or at the base of a tree. Common summer resident that nests throughout the Dakotas. More conspicuous during migration. Most arrive in April to May, and leave by September.

male

female

DOWNY WOODPECKER
Picoides pubescens

Size: 6" (15 cm)

Male: A small woodpecker with an all-white belly, black-and-white spotted wings, a black line running through the eyes, a short black bill, a white stripe down the back and red mark on the back of the head. Several small black spots along the sides of white tail.

Female: same as male, but lacks a red mark on head

Juvenile: same as female, some have a red mark near the forehead

Nest: cavity; male and female excavate; 1 brood per year

Eggs: 3-5; white without markings

Incubation: 11-12 days; female and male incubate, the female during day, male at night

Fledging: 20-25 days; male and female feed young

Migration: non-migrator

Food: insects, seeds; visits seed and suet feeders

Compare: Almost identical to the Hairy Woodpecker (pg. 37), but smaller. Look for the shorter, thinner bill of Downy to differentiate them.

Stan's Notes: This is one of the most abundant, widespread wood-peckers in the Dakotas, found throughout where trees are present. Stiff tail feathers help brace it like a tripod as it clings to a tree. Like all other woodpeckers, it has a long barbed tongue to pull insects from tiny places. Male and female drum on branches or hollow logs to announce territories, which are rarely larger than 5 acres (2 ha). Male performs most of the brooding. Will winter roost in cavity.

female pg. 101

breeding male

non-breeding male

SUMMER

LARK BUNTING
Calamospiza melanocorys

Size: 6½" (16 cm)

Male: Short, stocky black bird with a large broad head, white wing patches and large bluish gray bill. Winter is black, brown, gray and white-striped, with white wing patches.

Female: overall brown with a heavily streaked chest, white belly, black vertical line on each side of white chin, may have a dark central spot on the chest, faint white eyebrows

Juvenile: similar to adult of the same sex

Nest: cup; female builds; 1-2 broods per year

Eggs: 4-6; pale blue with markings

Incubation: 11-13 days; female and male incubate

Fledging: 8-12 days; female and male feed young

Migration: complete, to southwestern states, Mexico

Food: insects, seeds

Compare: The breeding male's bold black and white plumage is hard to confuse with any other bird's. Look for the rather large broad head and large bill to help identify.

Stan's Notes: Common throughout, but is more abundant in the western third of the Dakotas in dry plains and sagebrush regions. Has short rounded wings. Flying with shallow wing beats, the male flashes white wing patches. Male takes to air to display to female, setting its wings in a V position and floating back, rocking like a butterfly, singing a most amazing song. Song is like the song of Old World larks, hence the common name. Will flock with hundreds, if not thousands, of other Lark Buntings in autumn for migration.

breeding male

winter
male

female

SNOW BUNTING
Plectrophenax nivalis

Size: 7" (18 cm)

Male: Winter (September to March) chin, breast and belly are white. Has a rust brown head, back and shoulders. Small yellow bill. Black legs and feet. Breeding is overall white with black and white wings.

Female: similar to breeding male, but lacks the all-white head

Juvenile: similar to winter male

Nest: cavity; female builds; 1-2 broods per year

Eggs: 4-7; green to blue with brown markings

Incubation: 10-16 days; female incubates

Fledging: 10-17 days; male and female feed young

Migration: complete, to northern states

Food: insects, seeds

Compare: This bird is easy to identify since no other small sparrow-like bird has so much white.

Stan's Notes: A winter resident of the Dakotas. Usually is seen in flocks of up to 30 individuals of mixed ages and sexes. Appearing slightly different from each other, some are completely black and white, while others have a combination of black, white, brown and rust. Often feeds on the ground along roads. Sometimes seen with other winter birds such as Horned Larks and Lapland Longspurs. Female constructs a grass and moss nest in a cavity or on a cliff that is well protected from the weather. Young hatch at different times, so some leave the nest before others. Doesn't nest in the Dakotas.

female
pg. 111

male

ROSE-BREASTED GROSBEAK
Pheucticus ludovicianus

Size: 7-8" (18-20 cm)

Male: A plump black-and-white bird with a large, triangular rose patch in the center of chest. Wing linings are rosy red. Large ivory bill.

Female: heavily streaked brown and white bird with large white eyebrows, orange yellow wing linings

Juvenile: same as female

Nest: cup; the female and male build; 1-2 broods per year

Eggs: 3-5; blue green with brown markings

Incubation: 13-14 days; female and male incubate

Fledging: 9-12 days; female and male feed young

Migration: complete, to Mexico, Central America and South America

Food: insects, seeds, fruit; comes to seed feeders

Compare: Male is very distinctive with no look-alikes.

Stan's Notes: A summer resident, but more conspicuous when in small groups during spring and autumn migrations. Often prefers mature deciduous forest for nesting. Both sexes sing, but the male sings much louder and clearer. Has a rich, robin-like song. The name "Grosbeak" refers to its large bill, used to crush seeds. Rose breast patch varies in size and shape in each male. Late to arrive in spring and early to leave in autumn. Males arrive in small groups first, joined by females several days later. Several males can be seen visiting seed feeders at the same time in spring. When the females arrive, males become territorial and reduce their visits to feeders. Young grosbeaks visit feeders with adults after fledging.

male

female

HAIRY WOODPECKER
Picoides villosus

Size: 9" (22.5 cm)

Male: Black-and-white woodpecker with a white belly, and black wings with rows of white spots. White stripe down back. Long black bill. Red mark on back of head.

Female: same as male, but lacks a red mark on head

Juvenile: grayer version of female

Nest: cavity; female and male excavate; 1 brood per year

Eggs: 3-6; white without markings

Incubation: 11-15 days; female and male incubate, the female during day, male at night

Fledging: 28-30 days; male and female feed young

Migration: non-migrator

Food: insects, nuts, seeds; comes to seed and suet feeders

Compare: Larger than Downy Woodpecker (pg. 29), Hairy has a longer bill and lacks Downy's black spots along tail.

Stan's Notes: A common woodpecker of wooded backyards that announces its arrival with a sharp chirp before landing on feeders. This bird is responsible for eating many destructive forest insects. Has a barbed tongue, which helps it extract insects from trees. Tiny bristle-like feathers at the base of bill protect the nostrils from wood dust. Drums on hollow logs, branches or stovepipes in springtime to announce its territory. Often prefers to excavate nest cavities in live aspen trees. Has a larger, more oval-shaped cavity entrance than that of Downy Woodpecker.

SUMMER

RED-HEADED WOODPECKER
Melanerpes erythrocephalus

Size: 9" (22.5 cm)

Male: All-red head and a solid black back. White rump, chest and belly. Large white patches on wings flash when in flight. A black tail. Gray legs and bill.

Female: same as male

Juvenile: gray brown with white chest, lacks any red

Nest: cavity; male builds with help from female; 1 brood per year

Eggs: 4-5; white without markings

Incubation: 12-13 days; female and male incubate

Fledging: 27-30 days; female and male feed young

Migration: partial migrator to non-migrator; will move to areas with abundant supply of nuts

Food: insects, nuts, fruit; comes to seed and suet feeders

Compare: No other woodpecker in the Dakotas has an all-red head.

Stan's Notes: One of the few woodpecker species in which male and female appear the same (look alike). Bill is not as well adapted for excavating holes as in other woodpeckers, so it chooses dead or rotten tree branches for nest. Prefers more open or edge woodlands with many dead trees. Often seen perching on tops of dead snags. Stores acorns and other nuts. Decreasing populations nationwide.

female pg. 157

male

LESSER SCAUP
Aythya affinis

MIGRATION
SUMMER

Size: 16-17" (40-43 cm)

Male: Appears mostly black with bold white sides and gray back. Chest and head look nearly black, but head appears purple with green highlights in direct sun. Bright yellow eyes.

Female: overall brown with dull white patch at base of light gray bill, yellow eyes

Juvenile: same as female

Nest: ground; female builds; 1 brood per year

Eggs: 8-14; olive buff without markings

Incubation: 22-28 days; female incubates

Fledging: 45-50 days; female teaches young to feed

Migration: complete, southern states, Mexico, Central America and northern South America

Food: aquatic plants and insects

Compare: Larger than American Coot (pg. 19), which lacks male Scaup's white sides. Look for the distinctive white sides of the male Scaup to help identify. The male Blue-winged Teal (pg. 155) is smaller and has a bright white crescent-shaped patch near base of bill.

Stan's Notes: A summer resident in North Dakota. Seen in South Dakota during migration. Often seen in large flocks on lakes, ponds and sewage lagoons during migration. Completely submerges itself to feed on the bottom of lakes (unlike dabbling ducks, which only tip forward to reach bottom). Note the bold white stripe under the wings when in flight. Has an interesting baby-sitting arrangement in which groups of young are tended by one to three adult females.

winter

breeding

AMERICAN AVOCET
Recurvirostra americana

SUMMER

Size: 18" (45 cm)

Male: Black and white back, white belly. A long, thin upturned bill and long gray legs. Head and neck rusty red during breeding, gray in the winter.

Female: similar to male, only with a more strongly upturned bill

Juvenile: similar to adults, with a slight wash of rusty red on neck and head

Nest: ground; the female and male build; 1 brood per year

Eggs: 3-5; light olive with brown markings

Incubation: 22-29 days; female and male incubate

Fledging: 28-35 days; female and male feed young

Migration: complete, to southwestern states, Mexico

Food: insects, crustaceans, aquatic vegetation and fruit

Compare: One of the few long-legged shorebirds in the Dakotas. Look for the rusty red head of the breeding Avocet and long upturned bill.

Stan's Notes: A handsome long-legged bird that prefers shallow alkaline, saline or brackish water, it is well adapted to arid western U.S. conditions. Uses its up-curved bill to sweep from side to side across mud bottoms in search of insects. Both the male and female have a brood patch to incubate eggs and brood their young. Nests throughout the Dakotas in loose colonies of up to 20 pairs. All members of the colony will defend together against intruders.

43

male

female pg. 163

COMMON GOLDENEYE
Bucephala clangula

**SUMMER
WINTER**

Size: 18½-20" (47-50 cm)

Male: A mostly white duck with a black back and large, puffy green head. Large white spot in front of each bright golden eye. Dark bill.

Female: brown and gray, a large dark brown head, gray body, white collar, bright golden eyes, yellow-tipped dark bill

Juvenile: same as female, but has a dark bill

Nest: cavity; female lines old woodpecker cavity; 1 brood per year

Eggs: 8-10; light green without markings

Incubation: 28-32 days; female incubates

Fledging: 56-59 days; female leads young to food

Migration: complete, to southern states and Mexico; winters in parts of the Dakotas

Food: aquatic plants, insects

Compare: Similar to, but larger than, the black and white male Lesser Scaup (pg. 41). Look for the distinctive white mark in front of each golden eye, and a white chest.

Stan's Notes: Known for its loud whistling, produced by its wings in flight. In late winter and early spring, male often attracts female through elaborate displays, throwing its head backward while it utters a single raspy note. Female will lay eggs in other goldeneye nests, which results in some mothers incubating up to 30 eggs. Received the common name from its obvious bright golden eyes. Winters in the Dakotas where it finds open water.

YEAR-ROUND

BLACK-BILLED MAGPIE
Pica hudsonia

Size: 20" (50 cm)

Male: A large black-and-white bird with very long tail and white belly. Iridescent green wings and tail in direct sunlight. Large black bill and legs. White wing patches flash in flight.

Female: same as male

Juvenile: same as adult, but shorter tail

Nest: modified pendulous; the female and male build; 1 brood per year

Eggs: 5-8; green with brown markings

Incubation: 16-21 days; female incubates

Fledging: 25-29 days; female and male feed young

Migration: non-migrator

Food: insects, carrion, fruit, seeds

Compare: Contrasting black-and-white colors and the very long tail of Magpie distinguish it from the all-black American Crow (pg. 21).

Stan's Notes: A wonderfully intelligent bird that is able to mimic dogs, cats and even people. Will often raid a barnyard dog dish for food. Feeds on a variety of food from road kill to insects and seeds it collects from the ground. Easily identified by its bold black-and-white colors and long streaming tail. Travels in small flocks, usually family members, and tends to be very gregarious. Breeds in small colonies with unusual dome nest (dome-shaped roof) deep within thick shrubs. Will mate with same mate for several years. Prefers open fields with cattle or sheep, where it feeds on insects attracted to the livestock.

BLACK-CROWNED NIGHT-HERON
Nycticorax nycticorax

MIGRATION
SUMMER

Size: 22-27" (56-69 cm)

Male: A stocky, hunched and inactive heron with black back and crown, white belly and gray wings. Long dark bill, short yellow legs and bright red eyes. Breeding adult has two long white plumes on crown.

Female: same as male

Juvenile: golden brown head and back with white spots, streaked breast, yellow orange eyes, brown bill

Nest: platform; female and male build; 1 brood per year

Eggs: 3-5; light blue without markings

Incubation: 24-26 days; female and male incubate

Fledging: 42-48 days; female and male feed young

Migration: complete, to southern states, Mexico and Central America

Food: fish, aquatic insects

Compare: American Bittern (pg. 183) is overall brown and has a yellow bill. Half the size of Great Blue Heron (pg. 237) when perching. Look for a short-necked heron with a black back and crown.

Stan's Notes: A very secretive bird, this heron is most active near dawn and dusk (crepuscular). It hunts alone, but nests in small colonies. Roosts in trees during the day. Often squawks if disturbed from the daytime roost. Often seen being harassed by other herons during days.

rushing

weed dance

SUMMER

WESTERN GREBE
Aechmophorus occidentalis

Size: 24" (60 cm)

Male: A long-necked, nearly all-black water bird with white chin, neck, chest and belly. Long yellow bill and bright red eyes. Dark crown extends around eyes to base of bill. During winter, becomes light gray around eyes.

Female: same as male

Juvenile: similar to adult

Nest: platform; female and male build; 1 brood per year

Eggs: 3-4; bluish white with brown markings

Incubation: 20-23 days; female and male incubate

Fledging: 65-75 days; female and male feed young

Migration: complete, to western coastal U.S.

Food: fish, aquatic insects

Compare: A familiar long-necked water bird. Striking black and white plumage makes it hard to confuse with any other bird.

Stan's Notes: Well known for its unusual breeding dance known as rushing. Side by side, with necks outstretched, mates will spring to their webbed feet and dance across the water's surface (see inset), diving underwater at the end of the rush. Often holds long stalks of water plants in bill when courting mate, called the weed dance (see inset). Its legs are positioned far back on the body, making it difficult to walk on ground. Shortly after choosing a large lake for breeding and till late in summer, it rarely flies. Young ride on backs of adults, climbing on only minutes after hatching. Nests in large colonies of up to 100 pairs on lakes with lots of tall vegetation.

soaring

juvenile

BALD EAGLE
Haliaeetus leucocephalus

YEAR-ROUND
MIGRATION
WINTER

Size: 31-37" (79-94 cm); up to 7-foot wingspan

Male: Pure white head and tail contrast with dark brown-to-black body and wings. A large, curved yellow bill and yellow feet.

Female: same as male, only slightly larger

Juvenile: dark brown with white spots or speckles throughout body and wings, gray bill

Nest: massive platform, usually in a tree; female and male build; 1 brood per year

Eggs: 2; off-white without markings

Incubation: 34-36 days; female and male incubate

Fledging: 75-90 days; female and male feed young

Migration: non-migrator to partial, to southern states

Food: fish, carrion, birds (mainly ducks)

Compare: Larger than Turkey Vulture (pg. 23), which lacks adult Bald Eagle's white head and tail. Turkey Vulture has two-toned wings and flies with its wings in a V shape, unlike the straight-out wing position of the Eagle.

Stan's Notes: Driven to near extinction due to DDT poisoning and illegal killing. Now making a comeback in North America. Returns to same nest each year, adding more sticks, enlarging it to massive proportions, at times up to 1,000 pounds (450 kg). In the midair mating ritual, one eagle will flip upside down and lock talons with another. Both tumble, then break apart to continue flight. Thought to mate for life, but will switch mates if not successful reproducing. Juvenile attains the white head and tail at about 4 to 5 years of age.

female pg. 85

male

LAZULI BUNTING
Passerina amoena

Size: 5½" (14 cm)

Male: A turquoise blue head, neck, back and tail. Cinnamon chest with cinnamon extending down flanks slightly. White belly. Two bold white wing bars. Non-breeding male has a spotty blue head and back.

Female: overall grayish brown, warm brown breast, a light wash of blue on wings and tail, gray throat, a light gray belly, two narrow white wing bars

Juvenile: similar to adult of the same sex

Nest: cup; female builds; 2-3 broods per year

Eggs: 3-5; pale blue without markings

Incubation: 11-13 days; female incubates

Fledging: 10-12 days; female and male feed young

Migration: complete, to Mexico

Food: insects, seeds

Compare: Male Eastern Bluebird (pg. 61) is larger and lacks the male Bunting's white wing bars.

Stan's Notes: This bunting is more common in the western half of the Dakotas. Has a strong association with water such as rivers and streams. Doesn't like dense forests. After breeding, gathers in small flocks to hunt for insects and search for seeds. It has increased in population and expanded its range over the last century.

TREE SWALLOW
Tachycineta bicolor

SUMMER

Size: 5-6" (13-15 cm)

Male: Blue green in the spring and greener in fall. Appears to change color in direct sunlight. A white belly, a notched tail and pointed wing tips.

Female: similar to male, only duller

Juvenile: gray brown with a white belly and grayish breast band

Nest: cavity; female and male line former woodpecker cavity or nest box; 1 brood per year

Eggs: 4-6; white without markings

Incubation: 13-16 days; female incubates

Fledging: 20-24 days; female and male feed young

Migration: complete, to southern states, Mexico and Central America

Food: insects

Compare: Similar color to Purple Martin (pg. 65), but smaller and has white chest and belly. Barn Swallow (pg. 59) has rust belly and deeply forked tail.

Stan's Notes: This swallow is most common along ponds, lakes and agricultural fields. Attracted to your yard with a nesting box. Competes with Eastern Bluebirds for cavities and nest boxes. Will travel great distances to find dropped feathers to line its grass nest. Sometimes seen playing, chasing after dropped feathers. It is often seen flying back and forth across open fields, feeding on insects. Gathers in large flocks to migrate.

BARN SWALLOW
Hirundo rustica

Size: 7" (18 cm)

Male: A sleek swallow with a blue black back, a cinnamon belly and a reddish brown chin. White spots on long forked tail.

Female: same as male, only slightly duller

Juvenile: similar to adults, with a tan belly and chin, and shorter tail

Nest: cup; female and male build; 2 broods a year

Eggs: 4-5; white with brown markings

Incubation: 13-17 days; female incubates

Fledging: 18-23 days; female and male feed young

Migration: complete, to South America

Food: insects, prefers beetles, wasps and flies

Compare: Larger than Cliff Swallow (pg. 87), which lacks the distinctive, deeply forked tail. The Chimney Swift (pg. 71) has narrow pointed tail with wings longer than the body. Purple Martin (pg. 65) is nearly 2 inches (5 cm) larger and has a dark purple belly.

Stan's Notes: Of the six swallow species in the Dakotas, this is the only one with a deeply forked tail. Unlike other swallows, the Barn Swallow rarely glides in flight, so look for continuous flapping. It builds a mud nest using up to 1,000 beak-loads of mud, often in or on barns. Nests in colonies of four to six, but nesting alone is not uncommon. Drinks while flying by skimming water or getting water from wet leaves. It also bathes while flying through the rain or sprinklers.

EASTERN BLUEBIRD
Sialia sialis

Size: 7" (18 cm)

Male: Reminiscent of its larger cousin, American Robin, with a rusty red breast and a white belly. Sky blue head, back and tail.

Female: shares rusty red breast and white belly, but is grayer with faint blue tail and wings

Juvenile: similar to female, with spots on chest, blue wing markings

Nest: cavity, old woodpecker cavity or man-made nest box; female builds; 2 broods per year

Eggs: 4-5; pale blue without markings

Incubation: 12-14 days; female incubates

Fledging: 15-18 days; male and female feed young

Migration: complete, to southern states

Food: insects, fruit

Compare: Mountain Bluebird (pg. 63) is the same size, but lacks Eastern's rusty red breast. Blue Jay (pg. 67) is considerably larger, with a crest and white markings.

Stan's Notes: A summer resident of open fields and agricultural areas, gathering in large family groups for migration. Once nearly eliminated from the Dakotas due to a lack of nest cavities, bluebirds have made a remarkable comeback with the aid of bird enthusiasts who have put up thousands of bluebird boxes. Bluebirds like open fields, pastures, roadsides and other open habitats. Will perch in trees or on fence posts, waiting for grasshoppers and other insects. Gives a distinctive "chur-lee chur chur-lee" song. Young of the first brood help raise young of the second.

male

female

MOUNTAIN BLUEBIRD
Sialia currucoides

MIGRATION
SUMMER

Size: 7" (18 cm)

Male: An overall sky blue bird with a darker blue head, back, wings and tail and white lower belly. Thin black bill.

Female: similar to male, but paler with a nearly gray head and chest and a whitish belly

Juvenile: similar to adult of the same sex

Nest: cavity, old woodpecker cavity, wooden nest box; female builds; 1-2 broods per year

Eggs: 4-6; pale blue without markings

Incubation: 13-14 days; female incubates

Fledging: 22-23 days; female and male feed young

Migration: complete, to Arizona, California, Mexico

Food: insects

Compare: Similar to Eastern Bluebird (pg. 61), but lacks Eastern's rusty red breast.

Stan's Notes: Common in open country, nesting in the western Dakotas. Due to conservation of suitable nest sites (dead trees with cavities and man-made nesting boxes), populations have increased dramatically over the past 50 years. Like other bluebirds, Mountain Bluebirds take well to nesting boxes and tolerate close contact with humans. Young will imprint on their first nesting box or cavity, then choose a similar type of box or cavity throughout the rest of life.

PURPLE MARTIN
Progne subis

**MIGRATION
SUMMER**

Size: 8½" (22 cm)

Male: A large swallow-shaped bird with a purple head, back and belly. Black wings and tail. Notched tail.

Female: gray purple head and back with a whitish belly, darker wings and tail

Juvenile: same as female

Nest: cavity; female and male line the cavity of house; 1 brood per year

Eggs: 4-5; white without markings

Incubation: 15-18 days; female incubates

Fledging: 26-30 days; male and female feed young

Migration: complete, to South America

Food: insects

Compare: The male is the only swallow with a dark purple belly. Usually only seen in groups.

Stan's Notes: The largest swallow species in North America. Once nested in tree cavities in the Dakotas, but now nearly exclusively nests in man-made nesting boxes. Main diet consists of dragonflies, not mosquitoes as once thought. Often drinks and bathes while flying by skimming water or flying through rain. Returns to the same nest site each year. Males arrive before females and yearlings. Often nests within 100 feet (30 m) of a human dwelling and, in fact, the most successful colonies are located within this distance. Young strike out to form new colonies. Huge colonies gather in the fall to migrate to South America.

BLUE JAY
Cyanocitta cristata

Size: 12" (30 cm)

Male: Large bright-light-blue and white bird with black necklace. Crest moves up and down at will. White face with a gray belly. White wing bars on blue wings. Black spots and a white tip on blue tail.

Female: same as male

Juvenile: same as adult, only duller

Nest: cup; the female and male build; 1-2 broods per year

Eggs: 4-5; green to blue with brown markings

Incubation: 16-18 days; female incubates

Fledging: 17-21 days; female and male feed young

Migration: non-migrator to partial migrator; will move around to find abundant food source

Food: insects, fruit, carrion, seeds, nuts; comes to seed feeders, and ground feeders with corn

Compare: Eastern Bluebird (pg. 61) is much smaller and lacks the crest. The Belted Kingfisher (pg. 69) lacks the vivid blue coloring and black necklace of Blue Jay.

Stan's Notes: Highly intelligent bird, solving problems, gathering food and communicating more than other birds. Will scream like a hawk to scatter birds at a feeder before approaching. Known as the alarm of the forest, screaming at any intruders in the woods. Is known to eat eggs or young birds from nests of other birds. One of the few birds to cache food. Feathers don't contain blue pigment; refracted sunlight casts blue light.

male

female

BELTED KINGFISHER
Ceryle alcyon

YEAR-ROUND
SUMMER

Size: 13" (33 cm)

Male: Large blue bird with white belly. Broad blue gray breast band and a ragged crest that is raised and lowered at will. Large head with a long, thick black bill. A small white spot directly in front of red brown eyes. Black wing tips with splashes of white that flash when flying.

Female: same as male, but with rusty breast band in addition to blue gray band, and rusty flanks

Juvenile: similar to female

Nest: cavity; female and male excavate; 1 brood per year

Eggs: 6-7; white without markings

Incubation: 23-24 days; female and male incubate

Fledging: 23-24 days; female and male feed young

Migration: complete, to southern states, Mexico, and Central and South America

Food: small fish

Compare: Similar in size to the Blue Jay (pg. 67), but the Kingfisher is darker blue with a larger, more ragged crest.

Stan's Notes: Seen perched on branches near the water, it dives headfirst for small fish and returns to a branch to eat. Has a loud machine-gun-like call. Excavates a deep cavity in bank of river or lake. Parents drop dead fish into water, teaching the young to dive. Regurgitates pellets of bone after meals, being unable to pass bones through digestive tract. Mates recognize each other by call.

69

SUMMER

CHIMNEY SWIFT
Chaetura pelagica

Size: 5" (13 cm)

Male: Nondescript, swallow-shaped bird, usually only seen flying. Long, thin all-brown body with a pointed tail and head. Long swept-back wings are longer than body.

Female: same as male

Juvenile: same as adult

Nest: half cup; female and male build; 1 brood per year

Eggs: 4-5; white without markings

Incubation: 19-21 days; female and male incubate

Fledging: 28-30 days; female and male feed young

Migration: complete, to South America

Food: insects caught in air

Compare: Considerably smaller than Purple Martin (pg. 65) and lacks the iridescent purple of the Martin. Barn Swallow (pg. 59) has a forked tail, compared with the pointed tail of Chimney Swift.

Stan's Notes: One of the fastest fliers in the bird world. Spends all day flying, rarely perching. Bathes and drinks by skimming across water surfaces. Unique in-flight twittering call is often heard before bird is seen. Flies in groups, feeding on flying insects nearly 100 feet (30 m) in the air. Often called Flying Cigar due to its pointed body shape. Hundreds will nest and roost in large chimneys, hence the common name. Builds nest with tiny twigs, cementing it with saliva, attaching it to inside of chimney or hollow tree.

male

female

WINTER

COMMON REDPOLL
Carduelis flammea

Size: 5" (13 cm)

Male: A small sparrow-like bird with a bright red crown and black spot on the chin. Heavily streaked back and a splash of raspberry red on the chest.

Female: same as male, but lacking raspberry red on the chest

Juvenile: browner than adults, lacks a red crown, has dark streaks on the chest

Nest: cup; female builds; 1 brood (sometimes 2) per year

Eggs: 4-5; pale green with purple markings

Incubation: 10-11 days; female incubates

Fledging: 11-12 days; female and male feed young

Migration: irruptive; moves from Canada into North and South Dakota in some winters

Food: seeds, insects; will come to seed feeders

Compare: Slightly smaller than the male Purple Finch (pg. 255), lacking male Purple Finch's red back and rump. Similar to the male House Finch (pg. 253), but lacks the orange red rump. Look for the bright red crown and black spot under the bill.

Stan's Notes: Name is derived from the color and "taking a poll" or counting heads. After summering in the far reaches of Canada, it winters in the Dakotas. Winter flocks of up to 100 individuals are not uncommon. Bathes in snow or open water in winter. Much like the Black-capped Chickadee, it can be tamed and hand fed.

CHIPPING SPARROW
Spizella passerina

SUMMER

Size: 5" (13 cm)

Male: Small gray brown sparrow with a clear gray chest, rusty crown, white eyebrows with a black eye line, thin gray black bill and two faint wing bars.

Female: same as male

Juvenile: similar to adult, has a streaked breast, lacks the rusty crown

Nest: cup; female builds; 2 broods per year

Eggs: 3-5; blue green with brown markings

Incubation: 11-14 days; female incubates

Fledging: 10-12 days; female and male feed young

Migration: complete, to southern states, Mexico and Central America

Food: insects, seeds; will come to ground feeders

Compare: Similar to American Tree Sparrow (pg. 91), which shares a rusty crown, but lacks dark eye line. The larger Lark Sparrow (pg. 103) has a white chest and central spot. Smaller than the Song Sparrow (pg. 89), which has a heavily streaked chest. The female House Finch (pg. 79) also has a streaked chest.

Stan's Notes: A common garden or yard bird, often seen feeding on dropped seeds below feeders. Gathers in large family groups in autumn to feed in preparation for migration. Migrates during the night in flocks of 20 to 30 birds. Received its common name from the male's fast "chip" call. Often just called Chippy. Nest is placed low in dense shrubs and is almost always lined with animal hair.

PINE SISKIN
Carduelis pinus

Size: 5" (13 cm)

Male: Small brown finch. Heavily streaked back, breast and belly. Yellow wing bars. Yellow at base of tail. Thin bill.

Female: same as male

Juvenile: similar to adult, light yellow tinge over the breast and chin

Nest: modified cup; the female builds; 2 broods per year

Eggs: 3-4; greenish blue with brown markings

Incubation: 12-13 days; female incubates

Fledging: 14-15 days; female and male feed young

Migration: irruptive; moves around North and South Dakota in search of food

Food: seeds, insects; will come to seed feeders

Compare: Female American Goldfinch (pg. 277) lacks streaks and has white wing bars. Female House Finch (pg. 79) has a streaked chest, but lacks yellow wing bars. Female Purple Finch (pg. 95) has bold white eyebrows.

Stan's Notes: Usually considered a winter finch, seen in flocks of up to 20 individuals, often with other finch species. While it can be found throughout the Dakotas in heavy invasion years, it is absent in many winters. Will come to thistle feeders. Travels and breeds in small groups. Male feeds the female during incubation. Juveniles lose yellow tint by late summer of the first year. Builds its nest toward ends of coniferous branches, where needles are dense, helping to conceal. Nests are often only a few feet apart.

male pg. 253

female

HOUSE FINCH
Carpodacus mexicanus

YEAR-ROUND

Size: 5" (13 cm)

Female: A plain brown bird with a heavily streaked white chest.

Male: orange red face, chest and rump, a brown cap, brown marking behind eyes, brown wings streaked with white, streaked belly

Juvenile: similar to female

Nest: cup, sometimes in cavities; female builds; 2 broods per year

Eggs: 4-5; pale blue, lightly marked

Incubation: 12-14 days; female incubates

Fledging: 15-19 days; female and male feed young

Migration: non-migrator to partial migrator; will move around to find food

Food: seeds, fruit, leaf buds; will visit seed feeders

Compare: The female Purple Finch (pg. 95) is very similar, but has bold white eyebrows. The female American Goldfinch (pg. 277) has a clear chest and white wing bars. Similar to Pine Siskin (pg. 77), but lacks yellow wing bars and has a much larger bill than Siskin.

Stan's Notes: Very social bird. Visits feeders in small flocks. Likes nesting in hanging flower baskets. Incubating female is fed by the male. Has a loud, cheerful warbling song. House Finches that were originally introduced to Long Island, New York, from the western U.S. in the 1940s have since populated the entire eastern U.S. Now found throughout the country. Suffers from a fatal eye disease that causes eyes to crust over.

HOUSE WREN
Troglodytes aedon

SUMMER

Size: 5" (13 cm)

Male: A small all-brown bird with lighter brown markings on tail and wings. Slightly curved brown bill. Often holds its tail erect.

Female: same as male

Juvenile: same as adult

Nest: cavity; female and male line just about any nest cavity; 2 broods per year

Eggs: 4-6; tan with brown markings

Incubation: 10-13 days; female and male incubate

Fledging: 12-15 days; female and male feed young

Migration: complete, to southern states and Mexico

Food: insects

Compare: Wren's long curved bill and long upturned tail differentiates it from sparrows. Lack of eyebrows distinguishes it from other wrens.

Stan's Notes: A prolific songster, it will sing from dawn until dusk during the mating season. Easily attracted to nest boxes. In spring, the male chooses several prospective nesting cavities and places a few small twigs in each. Female inspects each, chooses one, and finishes the nest building. She will completely fill the nest cavity with uniformly small twigs, then line a small depression at back of cavity with pine needles and grass. Often has trouble fitting long twigs through nest cavity hole. Tries many different directions and approaches until successful.

male pg. 201

female

WINTER

DARK-EYED JUNCO
Junco hyemalis

Size: 5½" (14 cm)

Female: A round, dark-eyed bird with tan-to-brown chest, head and back. White belly. Ivory-to-pink bill. Since the outermost tail feathers are white, tail appears as a white V in flight.

Male: same as female, only slate gray to charcoal

Juvenile: similar to female, but has a streaked breast and head

Nest: cup; female and male build; 2 broods a year

Eggs: 3-5; white with reddish brown markings

Incubation: 12-13 days; female incubates

Fledging: 10-13 days; male and female feed young

Migration: complete, throughout the U.S.; winters in the Dakotas

Food: seeds, insects; will come to seed feeders

Compare: Rarely confused with any other bird. Small flocks feed under bird feeders in winter.

Stan's Notes: Common in winter, this bird is usually seen on the ground in small flocks. It adheres to a rigid social hierarchy, with dominant birds chasing less dominant birds. Look for white outer tail feathers flashing while it is in flight. Most comfortable on the ground, juncos will "double-scratch" with both feet to expose seeds and insects. Consumes many weed seeds. Several junco species have now been combined into one, simply called Dark-eyed Junco. Doesn't nest in the Dakotas.

male pg. 55

female

LAZULI BUNTING
Passerina amoena

Size: 5½" (14 cm)

Female: Overall grayish brown with a warm brown chest, light wash of blue on wings and tail, gray throat and light gray belly. Two narrow white wing bars.

Male: turquoise blue head, neck, back and tail, cinnamon chest, white belly and two bold white wing bars

Juvenile: similar to adult of the same sex

Nest: cup; female builds; 2-3 broods per year

Eggs: 3-5; pale blue without markings

Incubation: 11-13 days; female incubates

Fledging: 10-12 days; female and male feed young

Migration: complete, to Mexico

Food: insects, seeds

Compare: Female Mountain Bluebird (pg. 63) is larger and has much more blue than the female Lazuli Bunting.

Stan's Notes: This bunting is more common in the western half of the Dakotas. Has a strong association with water such as rivers and streams. Doesn't like dense forests. After breeding, gathers in small flocks to hunt for insects and search for seeds. It has increased in population and expanded its range over the last century.

CLIFF SWALLOW
Petrochelidon pyrrhonota

SUMMER

Size: 5½" (14 cm)

Male: A uniquely patterned swallow with a dark back, wings and cap. Distinctive tan-to-rust rump, cheeks and forehead.

Female: same as male

Juvenile: similar to adult, lacks distinct patterning

Nest: gourd-shaped, made of mud; the male and female build; 1-2 broods per year

Eggs: 3-6; pale white with brown markings

Incubation: 14-16 days; male and female incubate

Fledging: 21-24 days; female and male feed young

Migration: complete, to South America

Food: insects

Compare: Barn Swallow (pg. 59) is larger and has a blue back and wings and deeply forked tail.

Stan's Notes: A common and widespread swallow species in the Dakotas during the summer. Common around bridges (especially bridges over water) and rural housing (especially in open country near cliffs). Builds a gourd-shaped nest with a funnel-like entrance pointing down. A colony nester, with many nests lined up beneath eaves of buildings or under cliff overhangs. Will carry balls of mud up to a mile to construct its nest. Many of the colony return to the same nest sites each year. Not unusual for it to have two broods per season. If the number of nests beneath eaves becomes a problem, wait until after young have left the nests to hose off the mud.

SONG SPARROW
Melospiza melodia

Size: 5-6" (13-15 cm)

Male: Common brown sparrow with heavy dark streaks on breast coalescing into a central dark spot.

Female: same as male

Juvenile: similar to adult, finely streaked breast, lacks a central spot

Nest: cup; female builds; 2 broods per year

Eggs: 3-4; pale blue to green with reddish brown markings

Incubation: 12-14 days; female incubates

Fledging: 9-12 days; female and male feed young

Migration: complete, southern states, non-migrator in South Dakota and southern North Dakota

Food: insects, seeds; rarely visits seed feeders

Compare: Similar to other brown sparrows. Look for a heavily streaked chest with central dark spot.

Stan's Notes: Many Song Sparrow subspecies or varieties, but dark central spot carries through each variant. While the female builds another nest for a second brood, the male sparrow often takes over feeding the young. Returns to a similar area each year, defending a small territory by singing from thick shrubs. A common host of the Brown-headed Cowbird. Ground feeders, look for them to scratch simultaneously with both feet to expose seeds. Unlike many other sparrow species, Song Sparrows rarely flock together.

side view

front view

AMERICAN TREE SPARROW
Spizella arborea

Size: 6" (15 cm)

Male: A common brown sparrow with tan breast and rusty crown. Black spot in the center of breast. Upper bill is dark, lower bill yellow. Two white wing bars. Gray eyebrows.

Female: same as male

Juvenile: lacks rusty crown, has streaked chest, often obscuring the central dark spot

Nest: cup; female builds; 1 brood per year

Eggs: 3-5; green white with brown markings

Incubation: 12-13 days; female incubates

Fledging: 8-10 days; female and male feed young

Migration: complete, across North America; winters in the Dakotas

Food: insects, seeds; visits seed feeders

Compare: Looks similar to other sparrows, so look closely at the center of the breast for the single dark spot. Shares a rusty crown with the Chipping Sparrow (pg. 75), but lacks Chippy's distinctive white eyebrows and black eye line. Song Sparrow (pg. 89) has a heavily streaked chest.

Stan's Notes: Commonly seen during spring and fall migrations in flocks ranging from 2 to 200. A bird feeder visitor in the Dakotas during winter. Occasionally called Winter Chippy because it looks similar to Chipping Sparrow, a summer visitor. Nests in northern Canada and Alaska.

YEAR-ROUND

HOUSE SPARROW
Passer domesticus

Size: 6" (15 cm)

Male: Medium sparrow-like bird with large black spot on throat extending down to the chest. Brown back and single white wing bars. A gray belly and crown.

Female: all-light-brown bird, slightly smaller, lacks the black throat patch and single wing bars

Juvenile: similar to female

Nest: domed cup nest, within cavity; female and male build; 2-3 broods per year

Eggs: 4-6; white with brown markings

Incubation: 10-12 days; female incubates

Fledging: 14-17 days; female and male feed young

Migration: non-migrator; moves around to find food

Food: seeds, insects, fruit; comes to seed feeders

Compare: Lacks the rusty crown of the American Tree Sparrow (pg. 91) and Chipping Sparrow (pg. 75). Harris's Sparrow (pg. 117) has a black "hood" and white chest. Look for the black bib of male and clear chest of female.

Stan's Notes: One of the first bird songs heard in cities in spring. Familiar city bird, nearly always in flocks. Introduced from Europe to Central Park, New York, in 1850 and now found throughout North America. These birds are not really sparrows, but members of the Weaver Finch family, characterized by their large, oversized domed nests. Constructs a nest containing scraps of plastic, paper and whatever else is available. An aggressive bird that will kill the young of other birds in order to take over a cavity.

male pg. 255

female

PURPLE FINCH
Carpodacus purpureus

MIGRATION
SUMMER
WINTER

Size: 6" (15 cm)

Female: A plain brown bird with a heavily streaked chest. Prominent white eyebrows.

Male: raspberry red head, cap, breast, back and rump, brownish wings and tail

Juvenile: same as female

Nest: cup; female and male build; 1 brood a year

Eggs: 4-5; greenish blue with brown markings

Incubation: 12-13 days; female incubates

Fledging: 13-14 days; female and male feed young

Migration: irruptive; moves around in search of food

Food: seeds, insects, fruit; comes to seed feeders

Compare: Female House Finch (pg. 79) lacks female Purple Finch's white eyebrows. Pine Siskin (pg. 77) has yellow wing bars and a much smaller bill than Purple Finch. The female American Goldfinch (pg. 277) has a clear chest and white wing bars.

Stan's Notes: Usually only seen in the winter or during migration, when Purple Finches leave their northern homes and move around in search of food. Travels in flocks of up to 50. It is common in non-residential areas (prefers open woods or edges of woodland) and has been replaced in northern cities by House Finches. Feeds primarily on seeds, with seeds of ash trees a very important food source. Will visit seed feeders along with House Finches, making it hard to tell them apart. Has a rich loud song, with a distinctive "tic" note made only in flight. Not a purple color, the Latin species name *purpureus* means "crimson" or other reddish color.

breeding
male

female

CHESTNUT-COLLARED LONGSPUR
Calcarius ornatus

Size: 6" (15 cm)

Male: Breeding plumage (March to September) is overall brown. Head striped with black and white. Rusty red nape "collar." Dull yellow throat. Black chest and belly. Small pointed bill. Winter much duller. Lacks black head stripes, black chest and belly and red nape.

Female: similar to winter male, lacks the black and white head, black chest and belly, red nape

Juvenile: similar to female, but duller

Nest: cup; female builds; 1-2 broods per year

Eggs: 3-6; white with brown markings

Incubation: 10-13 days; female incubates

Fledging: 9-14 days; male and female feed young

Migration: complete, to Texas and Mexico

Food: insects, seeds

Compare: The Lapland Longspur (pg. 99) is a winter visitor, while the Chestnut-collared visits in summer. The rusty red nape and black belly help to easily identify this grassland bird.

Stan's Notes: This bird is found in grasslands and native prairies throughout the Dakotas. Common name "Longspur" refers to the long rear toe and nail, which are nearly twice the length of the front two toes. The nest is well concealed in a shallow depression under dense vegetation on the ground, with the rim of nest flush with the ground. Male performs a mating flight with rapid wing beats and a soft song. Adults eat insects and seeds. Young are fed an insect diet. One of four longspur species in North America.

breeding
male

winter male

female

LAPLAND LONGSPUR
Calcarius lapponicus

Size: 6¼" (15.5 cm)

Male: Breeding plumage (March to September) is overall brown with a black head, throat and chest. Tan eyebrows. Rusty red nape. White belly. Small, pointed yellow bill with a black tip. Winter plumage is much duller. Lacks the black head, throat and chest.

Female: very similar to winter male

Juvenile: similar to female, but duller

Nest: cup; female builds; 1 brood per year

Eggs: 3-7; pale green with brown markings

Incubation: 12-13 days; female incubates

Fledging: 8-10 days; male and female feed young

Migration: complete, to central states from the East to West coasts

Food: insects, seeds

Compare: The Chestnut-collared Longspur (pg. 97) is a summer visitor, while the Lapland visits in winter.

Stan's Notes: Common winter bird in the Dakotas, usually found in open areas and along roads. Often seen in flocks with Horned Larks and Snow Buntings. Common name "Longspur" refers to the long rear toe and nail, which are nearly twice the length of the front two toes. Nests in a shallow depression on the ground in Alaska and Northwest Territories of Canada. One of the widest breeding ranges, extending around the world just south of the polar region (circumpolar). One of four longspur species in North America.

male pg. 31

female

non-breeding male

LARK BUNTING
Calamospiza melanocorys

SUMMER

Size: 6½" (16 cm)

Female: Brown bird with heavily streaked chest and a white belly. Black vertical line on each side of white chin. May have a central dark spot on the chest. Faint white eyebrows.

Male: black bird with a large broad head, white wing patches and large bluish gray bill

Juvenile: similar to adult of the same sex

Nest: cup; female builds; 1-2 broods per year

Eggs: 4-6; pale blue with markings

Incubation: 11-13 days; female and male incubate

Fledging: 8-12 days; female and male feed young

Migration: complete, to southwestern states, Mexico

Food: insects, seeds

Compare: Appears similar to open country sparrows. The female Red-winged Blackbird (pg. 125) lacks the white belly and chin.

Stan's Notes: Common throughout, but is more abundant in the western third of the Dakotas in dry plains and sagebrush regions. Has short rounded wings. Flying with shallow wing beats, the male flashes white wing patches. Male takes to air to display to female, setting its wings in a V position and floating back, rocking like a butterfly, singing a most amazing song. Song is like the song of Old World larks, hence the common name. Will flock with hundreds, if not thousands, of other Lark Buntings in autumn for migration.

LARK SPARROW
Chondestes grammacus

Size: 6½" (16 cm)

Male: All-brown bird with unique rust red, white and black head pattern. White breast with a central black spot. Gray rump and white edges to gray tail, as seen in flight.

Female: same as male

Juvenile: similar to adult, no rust red on head

Nest: cup, on the ground; female builds; 1 brood per year

Eggs: 3-6; pale white with brown markings

Incubation: 10-12 days; male and female incubate

Fledging: 10-12 days; female and male feed young

Migration: complete, coastal Mexico, Central America

Food: seeds, insects

Compare: The White-throated Sparrow (pg. 105) and the White-crowned Sparrow (pg. 107) both lack the Lark Sparrow's rust red pattern on the head and central spot on a white chest. Larger than the Chipping Sparrow (pg. 75), which has similar rusty color on head, but lacks Lark's white chest and central spot.

Stan's Notes: One of the larger sparrow species and one of the best songsters, also well known for its courtship strutting, chasing and lark-like flight pattern (rapid wing beats with tail spread). A bird of open fields, pastures and prairies, found throughout the Dakotas but more abundant in the western half. It is very common during migration, when large flocks congregate. Uses nest for several years if the first brood is successful.

white-striped

tan-striped

WHITE-THROATED SPARROW
Zonotrichia albicollis

Size: 6-7" (15-18 cm)

Male: A brown bird with gray tan chest and belly. Small yellow spot between the eyes (lore). Distinctive white or tan throat patch. White or tan stripes alternate with black stripes on crown. Color of the throat patch and crown stripes match.

Female: same as male

Juvenile: similar to adult, gray throat and eyebrows with heavily streaked chest

Nest: cup; female builds; 1 brood per year

Eggs: 4-6; color varies from greenish to bluish to creamy white with red brown markings

Incubation: 11-14 days; female incubates

Fledging: 10-12 days; female and male feed young

Migration: complete, to southern states and Mexico

Food: insects, seeds, fruit; visits ground feeders

Compare: White-crowned Sparrow (pg. 107) lacks the throat patch and yellow lore. Lark Sparrow (pg. 103) has a rust red pattern on the head and central black spot on a white chest.

Stan's Notes: There are two color variations (polymorphic) of the White-throated Sparrow: white-striped or tan-striped. Studies have indicated the white-striped adults tend to mate with the tan-striped birds. No indication why. A winter resident mostly in South Dakota that is more abundant during migration, when it can be seen at ground feeders. Nests are built on the ground beneath small trees in bogs and coniferous forests. Doesn't nest in the Dakotas.

juvenile

WHITE-CROWNED SPARROW
Zonotrichia leucophrys

Size: 6½-7½" (16-19 cm)

Male: A brown sparrow with a gray breast and a black-and-white striped crown. Small, thin pink bill.

Female: same as male

Juvenile: similar to adult, with brown stripes on the head instead of white

Nest: cup; female builds; 2 broods per year

Eggs: 3-5; color varies from greenish to bluish to whitish with red brown markings

Incubation: 11-14 days; female incubates

Fledging: 8-12 days; male and female feed young

Migration: complete, to southern states and Mexico

Food: insects, seeds, berries; visits ground feeders

Compare: The White-throated Sparrow (pg. 105) has a white or tan throat patch, and yellow spot between eyes and bill, with a blackish bill. The Lark Sparrow (pg. 103) has a rust red pattern on the head and central black spot on a white chest.

Stan's Notes: Seen in groups of up to 20 during migration, when it can be seen feeding underneath seed feeders. Males arrive before females and establish territories by singing from perches. Feeds on the ground, scratching backward with both feet simultaneously. Male takes most of the responsibility of raising young while female starts the second brood. Only 9 to 12 days separate broods. Doesn't nest in the Dakotas.

MIGRATION
SUMMER

SWAINSON'S THRUSH
Catharus ustulatus

Size: 7" (18 cm)

Male: Dusty brown head, back and wings. Brown smudges and spots, especially on its throat, chest and off-white belly. A small, thin two-toned bill, yellow under and black above.

Female: same as male

Juvenile: overall lighter than adult, with less distinct spots on chest

Nest: cup; female builds; 1 brood per year

Eggs: 3-5; pale blue with brown markings

Incubation: 12-14 days; female incubates

Fledging: 10-14 days; female and male feed young

Migration: complete, to Mexico, Central America and South America

Food: insects, fruit

Compare: Similar shape as American Robin (pg. 217), but is smaller and lacks the red breast.

Stan's Notes: A common thrush during spring and fall migrations, and a summer resident in parts of the Dakotas. Often is hard to see because most of the time it stays on the ground in thick vegetation. Song sounds like someone playing a flute. Feeds mostly on insects during spring and summer, adding fruit to its diet in late summer. Nests in shrubs or low in conifers, building a bulky nest consisting of grass, bark and moss, all glued together with mud.

female

male pg. 35

ROSE-BREASTED GROSBEAK
Pheucticus ludovicianus

Size: 7-8" (18-20 cm)

Female: Plump, heavily streaked brown and white bird with obvious white eyebrows. Orange yellow wing linings.

Male: black-and-white bird with large, triangular rose patch in center of chest, wing linings rosy red

Juvenile: same as female

Nest: cup; the female and male build; 1-2 broods per year

Eggs: 3-5; blue green with brown markings

Incubation: 13-14 days; female and male incubate

Fledging: 9-12 days; female and male feed young

Migration: complete, to Mexico, Central America and South America

Food: insects, seeds, fruit; comes to seed feeders

Compare: Female looks like a large sparrow. Female is larger and has a more distinctive eyebrow mark than female Purple Finch (pg. 95). The female House Finch (pg. 79) has no eyebrow mark.

Stan's Notes: A summer resident, but more conspicuous when in small groups during migration. It often prefers mature deciduous forest for nesting. Both sexes sing, but male sings much louder and clearer. "Grosbeak" refers to its large bill, used to crush seeds. Late to arrive in spring, early to leave in fall. Males arrive first, joined by females several days later. When females arrive, males reduce their visits to feeders. The young visit feeders with adults after fledging.

111

HORNED LARK
Eremophila alpestris

YEAR-ROUND

Size: 7-8" (18-20 cm)

Male: A sleek tan-to-brown bird. Black necklace with a yellow chin and black bill. Two tiny "horns" on top of the head can be difficult to see. Black tail with white outer feathers noticeable in flight.

Female: same as male, only duller, "horns" are even less noticeable

Juvenile: lacks the black markings and yellow chin, doesn't form "horns" until second year

Nest: ground; female builds; 2-3 broods per year

Eggs: 3-4; gray with brown markings

Incubation: 11-12 days; female incubates

Fledging: 9-12 days; female and male feed young

Migration: non-migrator to partial in the Dakotas

Food: seeds, insects

Compare: Smaller than Meadowlark (pg. 297), which shares the black necklace and yellow chin. Look for the black marks in front of eyes.

Stan's Notes: The only true lark native to North America. A year-round resident, moving around in winter to find food. Larks are birds of open ground. Common in rural areas, often seen in large flocks. Population increased in North America over the past 100 years due to clearing land for farming. May have up to three broods per year because they get such an early start. Females will perform a fluttering distraction display if the nest is disturbed. Females can renest about seven days after the brood fledges. The name "Lark" comes from the Middle English word *laverock*, or "a lark."

Bohemian
Waxwing

1 year old

YEAR-ROUND
WINTER

CEDAR WAXWING
Bombycilla cedrorum

Size: 7½" (19 cm)

Male: Very sleek-looking gray-to-brown bird with pointed crest, light yellow belly and bandit-like black mask. Tip of tail is bright yellow and the tips of wings look as if they have been dipped in red wax.

Female: same as male

Juvenile: grayish with a heavily streaked chest, lacks red wing tips, black mask and sleek look

Nest: cup; female and male build; 1 brood a year, occasionally 2

Eggs: 4-6; pale blue with brown markings

Incubation: 10-12 days; female incubates

Fledging: 14-18 days; female and male feed young

Migration: partial migrator; moves around to find food

Food: cedar cones, fruit, insects

Compare: Similar to its larger, less common cousin, Bohemian Waxwing (see inset), which has white on wings and rust under tail. The female Cardinal (pg. 123) has a large red bill.

Stan's Notes: The name is derived from its red wax-like wing tips and preference for eating small blueberry-like cones of the cedar. Mostly seen in flocks, moving from area to area, looking for berries. Wanders in winter to find available food supplies. Seen more often in winter because naked branches reveal its presence. Year-round resident in very low numbers. During summer, before berries are abundant, it feeds on insects. Spends most of its time at the tops of tall trees. Listen for the very high-pitched "sreee" whistling sounds it constantly makes. Obtains mask after first year.

115

MIGRATION
WINTER

HARRIS'S SPARROW
Zonotrichia querula

Size: 7½" (19 cm)

Male: A very large sparrow with various amounts of black on head, extending down the nape and face onto the chest. White belly. Brown back and wings. Pink bill and legs.

Female: same as male

Juvenile: similar to adult, lacks the black "hood" and spotted chest

Nest: cup, on the ground; unknown who builds; 1 brood per year

Eggs: 4-5; white with brown markings

Incubation: 13-14 days; female incubates

Fledging: 11-12 days; female and male feed young

Migration: complete, to southern states; winters in most of South Dakota

Food: insects, seeds, berries; visits ground feeders

Compare: The House Sparrow (pg. 93) lacks the black "hood" of Harris's Sparrow.

Stan's Notes: A large sparrow usually seen in small groups of up to ten birds scratching beneath seed feeders during migration and winter. Nests in northern Canada, returning to South Dakota and the central U.S. for winter. Recent studies show that a bird's status is dependent upon the amount of black on its "hood," not its age. The more black, the higher the status. Named after Edward Harris (1799-1863), a companion of John James Audubon.

male pg. 3

female

BROWN-HEADED COWBIRD
Molothrus ater

Size: 7½" (19 cm)

Female: Dull brown bird with no obvious markings. Pointed, sharp gray bill.

Male: glossy black bird, chocolate brown head

Juvenile: similar to female, only dull gray color and a streaked chest

Nest: no nest; lays eggs in nests of other birds

Eggs: 5-7; white with brown markings

Incubation: 10-13 days; host bird incubates eggs

Fledging: 10-11 days; host birds feed young

Migration: complete, to southern states

Food: insects, seeds; will come to seed feeders

Compare: Female Red-winged Blackbird (pg. 125) is slightly larger and has white eyebrows and a streaked chest. European Starling (pg. 5) has speckles and a shorter tail.

Stan's Notes: A member of the blackbird family. Of approximately 750 species of parasitic birds worldwide, this is the only parasitic bird in the Dakotas, laying eggs in host birds' nests, leaving others to raise its young. Cowbirds are known to have laid eggs in nests of over 200 species of birds. Some birds reject cowbird eggs, but most incubate them and raise the young, even to the exclusion of their own. Look for warblers and other birds feeding young birds twice their own size. At one time cowbirds followed bison to feed on insects attracted to the animals.

winter

breeding

SPOTTED SANDPIPER
Actitis macularius

SUMMER

Size: 8" (20 cm)

Male: Olive brown back. Long bill and long dull yellow legs. White line over eyes. Breeding plumage has black spots on a white chest and belly. Winter has a clear chest and belly.

Female: same as male

Juvenile: similar to winter adult, with a darker bill

Nest: ground; female and male build; 2 broods per year

Eggs: 3-4; brownish with brown markings

Incubation: 20-24 days; male incubates

Fledging: 17-21 days; male feeds young

Migration: complete, to southern states, Mexico, and Central and South America

Food: aquatic insects

Compare: Smaller than Lesser Yellowlegs (pg. 135). The Killdeer (pg. 137) has two black bands around neck. Look for Sandpiper to bob its tail up and down while standing. Look for breeding Spotted Sandpiper's black spots extending from chest to belly.

Stan's Notes: One of the few shorebirds that will dive underwater if pursued. Able to fly straight up out of the water. Flies with wings held in a cup-like arc, rarely lifting them above a horizontal plane. Constantly bobs its tail while standing and walks as if delicately balanced. Female mates with multiple males and lays eggs in up to five different nests. Male incubates and cares for young. In winter plumage, it lacks black spots on the chest and belly.

male pg. 259

female

juvenile

YEAR-ROUND

NORTHERN CARDINAL
Cardinalis cardinalis

Size: 8-9" (20-22.5 cm)

Female: Buff brown bird with tinges of red on crest and wings, a black mask and large red bill.

Male: red bird with a black mask extending from face down to chin and throat, large red bill and crest

Juvenile: same as female, but with a blackish gray bill

Nest: cup; female builds; 2-3 broods per year

Eggs: 3-4; bluish white with brown markings

Incubation: 12-13 days; female and male incubate

Fledging: 9-10 days; female and male feed young

Migration: non-migrator

Food: seeds, insects, fruit; comes to seed feeders

Compare: Cedar Waxwing (pg. 115) has a small dark bill. Female Cardinal appears similar to the juvenile Cardinal. Look for female's bright red bill.

Stan's Notes: A familiar backyard bird. Look for the male feeding female during courtship. Male feeds young of the first brood by himself while female builds second nest. The name comes from the Latin word *cardinalis*, which means "important." Very territorial in spring, it will fight its own reflection in a window. Non-territorial during winter, gathering in small flocks of up to 20 birds. Both the female and male sing and can be heard anytime of year. Listen for its "whata-cheer-cheer-cheer" territorial call in spring.

male pg. 8

female

YEAR-ROUND
SUMMER

RED-WINGED BLACKBIRD
Agelaius phoeniceus

Size: 8½" (22 cm)

Female: Heavily streaked brown bird with a pointed brown bill and white eyebrows.

Male: jet black bird with red and yellow patches on upper wings, pointed black bill

Juvenile: same as female

Nest: cup; female builds; 2-3 broods per year

Eggs: 3-4; bluish green with brown markings

Incubation: 10-12 days; female incubates

Fledging: 11-14 days; female and male feed young

Migration: complete to partial, southern states, Mexico and Central America; moves to find food

Food: seeds, insects; will come to seed feeders

Compare: Larger than female Brown-headed Cowbird (pg. 119) and smaller than female Yellow-headed Blackbird (pg. 133), both of which lack white eyebrows and streaks on chest. Thinner body than female Rose-breasted Grosbeak (pg. 111) and has a pointed bill.

Stan's Notes: One of the most widespread and numerous birds in the Dakotas. It is a sure sign of spring when Red-winged Blackbirds return to the marshes. Flocks of up to 100,000 birds have been reported. Males return before the females and defend territories by singing from tops of surrounding vegetation. Males repeat call from the tops of cattails while showing off their red and yellow wing bars (epaulets). Females choose mate and usually will nest over shallow water in thick stands of cattails. Red-wingeds feed mostly on seeds in fall and spring, switching to insects during summer.

male pg. 7

female

SPOTTED TOWHEE
Pipilo maculatus

MIGRATION
SUMMER

Size:	8½" (22 cm)
Female:	A brown head, dirty red-brown sides and a white belly. Multiple white spots on wings and sides. Long black tail with a white tip. Rich red eyes.
Male:	mostly black, lacking the brown head
Juvenile:	brown with a heavily streaked chest
Nest:	cup; female builds; 1-2 broods per year
Eggs:	3-5; white with brown markings
Incubation:	12-14 days; female and male incubate
Fledging:	10-12 days; female and male feed young
Migration:	partial migrator
Food:	seeds, fruit, insects
Compare:	Smaller than American Robin (pg. 217). Female Rose-breasted Grosbeak (pg. 111) has a streaked breast and white eyebrows.

Stan's Notes: Summer visitor in western and southern parts of the Dakotas and seen during migration. Found in a variety of habitats from thick brush and forest edges to suburban backyards. Often can be heard noisily scratching through dead leaves on the ground as it searches for food. While over 70 percent of its diet is plant material, it eats more insects in spring and summer. Well known to retreat from danger, walking away rather than taking to flight. Cup nest is nearly always on the ground underneath bushes, away from where male perches to sing. Song and plumage vary geographically and are not well studied or understood.

in flight

SUMMER

COMMON NIGHTHAWK
Chordeiles minor

Size: 9" (22.5 cm)

Male: A camouflaged brown and white bird with white chin. A distinctive white band across wings and the tail, seen only in flight.

Female: similar to male, but with tan chin, lacks the white tail band

Juvenile: similar to female

Nest: no nest; lays eggs on the ground, usually on rocks, or on rooftop; 1 brood per year

Eggs: 2; cream with lavender markings

Incubation: 19-20 days; female and male incubate

Fledging: 20-21 days; female and male feed young

Migration: complete, to South America

Food: insects caught in air

Compare: Much larger than Chimney Swift (pg. 71). Look for the obvious white wing band of Nighthawk in flight, and the characteristic flap-flap-flap-glide flight pattern.

Stan's Notes: Usually only seen flying at dusk or after sunset, but not uncommon for it to be sitting on a fence post, sleeping during the day. A very noisy bird, repeating a "peenting" call during flight. Alternates slow wing beats with bursts of quick wing beats. Prolific insect eater. Prefers gravel rooftops for nesting in cities and nests on the ground in country. Male's distinctive springtime mating ritual is a steep diving flight terminated with a loud popping noise. One of the first birds to migrate each fall, starting in August.

BURROWING OWL
Athene cunicularia

Size: 9½" (24 cm); up to 21-inch wingspan

Male: A brown owl with bold white spots, white belly and very long legs. Yellow eyes.

Female: same as male

Juvenile: same as adult, but belly is brown

Nest: cavity, former underground mammal den; female and male line den; 1 brood per year

Eggs: 6-11; white without markings

Incubation: 21-28 days; female incubates

Fledging: 25-28 days; female and male feed young

Migration: complete, to Mexico and Central America

Food: insects, mammals, lizards, birds

Compare: Smaller than Great Horned Owl (pg. 173) and lacking the feather tuft "horns." Spends most of the time on the ground, compared with the tree-loving Great Horned.

Stan's Notes: An owl of fields, open backyards, golf courses and airports. Nests in small family units or in small colonies. Takes over the underground dens of mammals, occasionally widening its den by kicking dirt backward. Lines den with cow pies, horse dung, grass and feathers. Some people have had success attracting these owls to their backyards by creating artificial dens. Often seen in the day, standing or sleeping around den entrance. Male brings food to incubating female, often moving family to a new den when young are just a few weeks old. Will bob head up and down while doing deep knee bends when agitated or threatened.

male pg. 13

female

YELLOW-HEADED BLACKBIRD
Xanthocephalus xanthocephalus

SUMMER

Size: 9-11" (22.5-28 cm)

Female: A large brown bird with a dull yellow head and chest. Slightly smaller than male.

Male: black bird with a lemon yellow head, chest and nape of neck, black mask and gray bill, white wing patches

Juvenile: similar to female

Nest: cup; female builds; 2 broods per year

Eggs: 3-5; greenish white with brown markings

Incubation: 11-13 days; female incubates

Fledging: 9-12 days; female feeds young

Migration: complete, to southern states and Mexico

Food: insects, seeds

Compare: Larger than female Red-winged Blackbird (pg. 125), which has white eyebrows and streaked chest.

Stan's Notes: Usually heard before seen, Yellow-headed Blackbird has a low, hoarse, raspy or metallic call. Nests in deep water marshes unlike its cousin, the Red-winged Blackbird, which prefers shallow water. The male gives an impressive mating display, flying with head drooped and feet and tail pointing down while steadily beating its wings. The female incubates alone and feeds between three to five young. Young keep low and out of sight for up to three weeks before starting to fly. Migrates in flocks of up to 200 with other blackbirds. Flocks made up mainly of males return first in late March and early April; females return later. Most colonies consist of 20 to 100 nests.

LESSER YELLOWLEGS
Tringa flavipes

MIGRATION

Size: 10-11" (25-28 cm)

Male: A typical sandpiper-type bird with a brown back and wings and lightly streaked white breast and belly. Thin, straight black bill. Long yellow legs.

Female: same as male

Juvenile: same as adult

Nest: ground; female builds; 1 brood per year

Eggs: 3-4; yellowish with brown markings

Incubation: 22-23 days; male and female incubate

Fledging: 18-20 days; male and female lead young to food

Migration: complete, to South America

Food: aquatic insects, tiny fish

Compare: Breeding Willet (pg. 151) is larger and has brown legs. Breeding Spotted Sandpiper (pg. 121) is smaller and has black spots on its chest.

Stan's Notes: Usually seen in large flocks, it combs shorelines and mud flats looking for aquatic insects. Most often seen in the head down, tail up position, walking along, looking to snatch up food. Uses its long straight bill to pluck insects and tiny fish from water. Very shy bird that quite often moves into the water prior to taking flight. Has a variety of "flight" notes that it gives when taking off. A member of the group of sandpipers called Tattlers, all of which scream alarm calls when taking flight. Nests on marshes in spruce forests of central Alaska and central Canada. The nest is a simple depression atop a mound of earth.

135

KILLDEER
Charadrius vociferus

SUMMER

Size: 11" (28 cm)

Male: An upland shorebird with two black bands around the neck like a necklace. A brown back and white belly. Bright reddish orange rump, visible in flight.

Female: same as male

Juvenile: similar to adult, with only one neck band

Nest: ground; male builds; 2 broods per year

Eggs: 3-5; tan with brown markings

Incubation: 24-28 days; male and female incubate

Fledging: 25 days; male and female lead their young to food

Migration: complete, to southern states, Mexico and Central America

Food: insects

Compare: The Spotted Sandpiper (pg. 121) is found around water and lacks the two neck bands of the Killdeer.

Stan's Notes: The only shorebird with two black neck bands. It is known for its broken wing impression, which draws intruders away from nest. Once clear of the nest, the Killdeer takes flight. Nests are only a slight depression in a gravel area, often very difficult to see. Young look like yellow cotton balls on stilts when first hatched, but quickly molt to appear similar to parents. Able to follow parents and peck for insects soon after birth. Is technically classified as a shorebird, but doesn't live at the shore. Often found in vacant fields or along railroads. Has a very distinctive "kill-deer" call.

SUMMER

BROWN THRASHER
Toxostoma rufum

Size: 11" (28 cm)

Male: A rusty red bird with long tail and heavily streaked breast and belly. Two white wing bars. Long curved bill. Bright yellow eyes.

Female: same as male

Juvenile: same as adult, but eye color is grayish

Nest: cup; female and male build; 2 broods a year

Eggs: 4-5; pale blue with brown markings

Incubation: 11-14 days; female and male incubate

Fledging: 10-13 days; female and male feed young

Migration: complete, to southern states

Food: insects, fruit

Compare: Slightly larger in size and similar in shape to the American Robin (pg. 217) and Gray Catbird (pg. 209), but the Thrasher has a streaked chest, rusty color and yellow eyes.

Stan's Notes: A prodigious songster, often in thick shrubs where it sings deliberate musical phrases, repeating each twice. Male has the largest documented song repertoire of all North American birds, with over 1,100 song types. Often seen quickly flying or running in and out of dense shrubs. Noisy feeding due to habit of turning over leaves, small rocks and branches. This bird is more abundant in the central Great Plains than anywhere else in North America.

male

female

YEAR-ROUND
SUMMER

AMERICAN KESTREL
Falco sparverius

Size: 10-12" (25-30 cm); up to 2-foot wingspan

Male: Rusty brown back and tail. A white breast with dark spots. Double black vertical lines on white face. Blue gray wings. Distinctive wide black band with a white edge on tip of rusty tail.

Female: similar to male, but slightly larger, has rusty brown wings and dark bands on tail

Juvenile: same as adult of the same sex

Nest: cavity; doesn't build a nest within; 1 brood per year

Eggs: 4-5; white with brown markings

Incubation: 29-31 days; male and female incubate

Fledging: 30-31 days; female and male feed young

Migration: non-migrator to partial migrator

Food: insects, small mammals and birds, reptiles

Compare: Similar to other falcons. Look for the two vertical black stripes on face of Kestrel. No other small bird of prey has rusty-colored back or tail.

Stan's Notes: Formerly called Sparrow Hawk due to its small size. Could be called Grasshopper Hawk because it eats many grasshoppers. Hovers near roads before diving for prey. Adapts quickly to a wooden nesting box. Has pointed swept-back wings, seen in flight. Perches nearly upright. Unusual raptor in that males and females have quite different markings. Watch for them to pump their tails up and down after landing on perches.

yellow-shafted
male

yellow-shafted
female

red-shafted
female

red-shafted
male

NORTHERN FLICKER
Colaptes auratus

YEAR-ROUND
SUMMER

Size: 12" (30 cm)

Male: Brown and black woodpecker with a large white rump patch visible only when flying. Black necklace above a speckled breast. Red spot on nape. Black or red mustache.

Female: same as male, but lacking a mustache

Juvenile: same as adult of the same sex

Nest: cavity; female and male excavate; 1 brood per year

Eggs: 5-8; white without markings

Incubation: 11-14 days; female and male incubate

Fledging: 25-28 days; female and male feed young

Migration: complete, to southern states, non-migrator in South Dakota and parts of North Dakota

Food: insects, especially ants and beetles

Compare: Flickers are the only brown-backed woodpeckers in the Dakotas.

Stan's Notes: The flicker is the only woodpecker to regularly feed on the ground, preferring ants and beetles. Produces antacid saliva to neutralize the acid defense of ants. Male usually selects nest site; takes up to 12 days to excavate. Some have had success attracting flickers to nesting boxes stuffed with sawdust. The yellow-shafted variety has golden yellow wing linings and tails. Red-shafteds are winter visitors in North Dakota and year-round residents in South Dakota. Black mustaches in male yellow-shafteds; red mustaches in male red-shafteds. Where ranges of these varieties overlap in South Dakota, hybrids occur with salmon-colored wing linings as a result. Undulates deeply in flight while giving loud "wacka-wacka" calls.

MOURNING DOVE
Zenaida macroura

Size: 12" (30 cm)

Male: Smooth fawn-colored dove with gray patch on the head. Iridescent pink, green around neck. A single black spot behind and below eyes. Black spots on wings and tail. Pointed wedge-shaped tail with white edges.

Female: similar to male, lacking iridescent pink and green neck feathers

Juvenile: spotted and streaked

Nest: platform; female and male build; 2 broods per year

Eggs: 2; white without markings

Incubation: 13-14 days; male and female incubate, the male during day, female at night

Fledging: 12-14 days; female and male feed young

Migration: partial migrator to non-migrator; will move around to find food

Food: seeds; will visit seed and ground feeders

Compare: Smaller than Rock Pigeon (pg. 221), lacking its wide range of color combinations.

Stan's Notes: Name comes from its mournful cooing. A ground feeder, its head bobs as it walks. One of the few birds to drink without lifting head, same as Rock Pigeon. Parents feed the young a regurgitated liquid called crop-milk for the first few days of life. Flimsy platform nest of twigs often falls apart in a storm. Wind rushing through wing feathers in flight creates a characteristic whistling sound.

UPLAND SANDPIPER
Bartramia longicauda

SUMMER

Size: 12" (30 cm)

Male: Overall brown shorebird. Long yellow legs, a short brown-tipped yellow bill and white belly. Appears to have a thin neck and small head in relationship to its body.

Female: same as male

Juvenile: similar to adult

Nest: ground; the female and male build; 1 brood per year

Eggs: 3-4; off-white with red markings

Incubation: 21-27 days; female and male incubate

Fledging: 30-31 days; female and male feed young

Migration: complete, to South America

Food: insects, seeds

Compare: The breeding Spotted Sandpiper (pg. 121) is smaller, has shorter legs and black spots on its white breast. Seen in very different habitats, the Spotted Sandpiper is almost always near water while Upland is in grassy meadows and prairies.

Stan's Notes: A shorebird of the dry grassland that is aptly named. Often seen standing on fence posts or other perches in a prairie or grassland habitat. Frequently found in prairies and grasslands that were burned, where foraging for food is easier. A true indicator of high-quality prairie habitat, this shorebird returns to a more watery habitat after breeding and just before migrating. Frequently holds its wings open over its back for several seconds just after landing. Formerly known as Upland Plover. Was hunted in the late 1800s.

147

PIED-BILLED GREBE
Podilymbus podiceps

SUMMER

Size: 13" (33 cm)

Male: Small brown water bird with a black chin and black ring around a thick, chicken-like ivory bill. Puffy white patch under the tail. Has an unmarked brown bill during winter (September to February).

Female: same as male

Juvenile: paler than adult, with white spots and gray chest, belly and bill

Nest: floating platform; female and male build; 1 brood per year

Eggs: 5-7; bluish white without markings

Incubation: 22-24 days; female and male incubate

Fledging: 22-24 days; female and male feed young

Migration: complete, to southern states, Mexico and Central America

Food: crayfish, aquatic insects, fish

Compare: The smallest brown water bird that dives underwater for long periods of time.

Stan's Notes: This common summer resident is often seen diving for food. It slowly sinks like a submarine if disturbed. Once called Hell-diver because of the length of time it can stay submerged. Can surface far away from where it went under. Builds platform nest on a floating mat in water. Particularly sensitive to pollution. Adapted well to life on water, with short wings, lobed toes, and legs set close to the rear of body. While swimming is easy, it is very awkward on land. "Grebe" probably came from the Old English *krib*, meaning "crest," a reference to the Great Crested Grebe found in Europe.

breeding

winter pg. 225

displaying

WILLET
Catoptrophorus semipalmatus

MIGRATION
SUMMER

Size: 15" (38 cm)

Male: Brown breeding plumage with a brown bill and legs. White belly. Distinctive black and white wing lining pattern, seen in flight or during display.

Female: same as male

Juvenile: similar to breeding adult, more tan in color

Nest: ground; female builds; 1 brood per year

Eggs: 3-5; olive green with dark markings

Incubation: 24-28 days; male and female incubate

Fledging: unknown days; female and male feed young

Migration: complete, to southern coastal states, coastal Central and South America

Food: aquatic insects

Compare: Larger than the Lesser Yellowlegs (pg. 135), which has yellow legs.

Stan's Notes: Common summer resident in the Dakotas, also seen during migration. Appearing a rich, warm brown during breeding season and rather plain gray in winter, it always has a striking black and white wing pattern when seen flying. Uses its black and white wing patches to display to mate. Named after the "pill-will-willet" call it gives during the breeding season. Gives a "kip-kip-kip" alarm call when it takes flight. Also nests in other western states, along the East coast and in Canada.

GREEN-WINGED TEAL
Anas crecca

Size: 15" (38 cm)

Male: A chestnut head with a dark green patch in back of eyes extending down to the nape of neck and outlined in white. Gray body with a butter yellow tail. Green speculum.

Female: light brown in color with black spots, green speculum, small black bill

Juvenile: same as female

Nest: ground; female builds; 1 brood per year

Eggs: 8-10; creamy white without markings

Incubation: 21-23 days; female incubates

Fledging: 32-34 days; female teaches young to feed

Migration: complete, to southern states, non-migrator in southern South Dakota

Food: aquatic plants and insects

Compare: Male Green-winged Teal is not as colorful as the male Wood Duck (pg. 241). Female Blue-winged Teal (pg. 155) is similar in size and has a slight white mark at base of bill.

Stan's Notes: A common summer duck, and a year-round resident in southern parts of South Dakota. It is one of the smallest dabbling ducks, tipping forward in water to glean aquatic plants and insects from the bottom of shallow ponds. This behavior makes it vulnerable to ingesting spent lead shot, which can cause death. It walks well on land and thus will feed in fields and woodlands, but returns to ponds. Known for its fast and agile flight, groups spin and wheel through the air in tight formation. Green speculum is most obvious when in flight.

153

female

male

SUMMER

BLUE-WINGED TEAL
Anas discors

Size: 15-16" (38-40 cm)

Male: Small, plain-looking brown duck speckled with black. A gray head with a large white crescent-shaped mark at base of bill. Black tail with small white patch. Blue wing patch (speculum) usually only seen in flight.

Female: duller version of male, lacks facial crescent mark and white patch on tail, showing only slight white at base of bill

Juvenile: same as female

Nest: ground; female builds; 1 brood per year

Eggs: 8-11; creamy white

Incubation: 23-27 days; female incubates

Fledging: 35-44 days; female feeds young

Migration: complete, to southern states, Mexico and Central America

Food: aquatic plants, seeds, aquatic insects

Compare: Male Blue-winged has a distinct white face marking. The female is nearly half the size of female Mallard (pg. 181) and is similar to female Wood Duck (pg. 161), but lacks Wood Duck's eye-ring and crest.

Stan's Notes: An early migrator in North and South Dakota. Most breeding birds here leave before other, more northern ducks pass through in autumn. Builds nest some distance from water. Female performs a distraction display to protect her nest and young. Male leaves the female near the end of incubation. Planting crops and cultivating to pond edges have caused a decline in population.

male pg. 41

female

LESSER SCAUP
Aythya affinis

MIGRATION
SUMMER

Size: 16-17" (40-43 cm)

Female: Overall brown duck with dull white patch at base of light gray bill. Yellow eyes.

Male: white and gray, the chest and head appear nearly black but head appears purple with green highlights in direct sun, yellow eyes

Juvenile: same as female

Nest: ground; female builds; 1 brood per year

Eggs: 8-14; olive buff without markings

Incubation: 22-28 days; female incubates

Fledging: 45-50 days; female teaches young to feed

Migration: complete, southern states, Mexico, Central America and northern South America

Food: aquatic plants and insects

Compare: Male Blue-winged Teal (pg. 155) is smaller, with a bright white crescent-shaped patch near base of bill. Smaller than female Wood Duck (pg. 161), which has white around the eyes, but lacks the white mark at base of bill. Look for the white patch at base of bill to help identify female Lesser Scaup.

Stan's Notes: A summer resident in North Dakota. Seen in South Dakota during migration. Often seen in large flocks on lakes, ponds and sewage lagoons during migration. Completely submerges itself to feed on the bottom of lakes (unlike dabbling ducks, which only tip forward to reach bottom). Note the bold white stripe under the wings when in flight. Has an interesting baby-sitting arrangement in which groups of young are tended by one to three adult females.

YEAR-ROUND

GREATER PRAIRIE-CHICKEN
Tympanuchus cupido

Size: 17" (43 cm)

Male: A chicken-like brown bird. White barring throughout. Short rounded tail, fans out for display. Orange-to-yellow patches (air sacs) on the sides of neck and bright orange-to-yellow eyebrows (combs) during display.

Female: similar to male, darker with a tan throat

Juvenile: similar to adults

Nest: ground; female builds; 1 brood per year

Eggs: 7-12; olive with brown markings

Incubation: 23-24 days; female incubates

Fledging: 7-10 days; female shows young what to eat

Migration: non-migrator; moves around to find food

Food: insects, seeds, fruit

Compare: Much smaller than Wild Turkey (pg. 189), which is much darker and has a longer tail and neck.

Stan's Notes: Market hunting and intensive agriculture practices have nearly eliminated this bird from much of its historical range. Efforts are now under way for recovery. The Dakotas are also home to Lesser Prairie Chickens (not shown), which are slightly smaller and grayer overall. Many males perform a loud animated dance (see displaying photo) together in spring in shorter grassy areas known as leks. They bow forward, inflating air sacs, fanning tails, stomping feet, giving a low moan (sounds like air blowing across the top of an open bottle). Females watch for males who perform the best, fly into the arena to mate, then go off to build a nest and lay eggs.

159

male pg. 241

female

WOOD DUCK
Aix sponsa

Size: 17-20" (43-50 cm)

Female: A small brown dabbling duck. Bright white eye-ring and a not-so-obvious crest. A blue patch on wing is often hidden.

Male: highly ornamented with a green head and crest patterned with white and black, rusty chest, white belly and red eyes

Juvenile: same as female

Nest: cavity; female lines old woodpecker cavity; 1 brood per year

Eggs: 10-15; creamy white without markings

Incubation: 28-36 days; female incubates

Fledging: 56-68 days; female teaches young to feed

Migration: complete, to southern states

Food: aquatic insects, plants, seeds

Compare: Smaller than the female Mallard (pg. 181) and similar to the female Blue-winged Teal (pg. 155). Mallard and Teal lack the female Duck's bright white eye-ring and crest.

Stan's Notes: A common duck of quiet, shallow backwater ponds. Nests in old woodpecker holes or in nest boxes. Often seen flying deep in forest or perched high on tree branches. Female takes flight with loud squealing call and enters nest cavity from full flight. Will lay eggs in a neighboring female nest (egg dumping), resulting in some clutches in excess of 20 eggs. Young stay in nest cavity only 24 hours after hatching, then jump from up to 30 feet (9 m) to the ground or water to follow their mother, never returning to the nest.

female

male pg. 45

SUMMER
WINTER

COMMON GOLDENEYE
Bucephala clangula

Size: 18½-20" (47-50 cm)

Female: A brown and gray duck with a large dark brown head and gray body. White collar. Bright golden eyes. Yellow-tipped dark bill.

Male: mostly white duck with a black back and a large, puffy green head, large white spot in front of each bright golden eye, dark bill

Juvenile: same as female, but has a dark bill

Nest: cavity; female lines old woodpecker cavity; 1 brood per year

Eggs: 8-10; light green without markings

Incubation: 28-32 days; female incubates

Fledging: 56-59 days; female leads young to food

Migration: complete, to southern states and Mexico; winters in parts of the Dakotas

Food: aquatic plants, insects

Compare: Similar to, but larger than, the brown and white female Lesser Scaup (pg. 157). Look for female Goldeneye's dark brown head and white collar.

Stan's Notes: Known for its loud whistling, produced by its wings in flight. In late winter and early spring, male often attracts female through elaborate displays, throwing its head backward while it utters a single raspy note. Female will lay eggs in other goldeneye nests, which results in some mothers incubating up to 30 eggs. Received the common name from its obvious bright golden eyes. Winters in the Dakotas where it finds open water.

male pg. 243

female

SUMMER

NORTHERN SHOVELER
Anas clypeata

Size: 20" (50 cm)

Female: Medium-sized brown duck speckled with black. Green speculum. An extraordinarily large spoon-shaped bill, almost always held pointed toward the water.

Male: same spoon-shaped bill, iridescent green head, rusty sides and white breast

Juvenile: same as female

Nest: ground; female builds; 1 brood per year

Eggs: 9-12; olive without markings

Incubation: 22-25 days; female incubates

Fledging: 30-60 days; female leads young to food

Migration: complete, to southern states, Mexico and Central America

Food: aquatic insects, plants

Compare: Similar color as female Mallard (pg. 181), but Mallard lacks the Shoveler's large bill. Larger than female Wood Duck (pg. 161) and lacks the white eye-ring. Look for the female Shoveler's large spoon-shaped bill to help identify.

Stan's Notes: One of several species of shoveler, so called because of the peculiarly shaped bill. The Northern Shoveler is the only species of these ducks in North America. Seen in small flocks of five to ten, swimming low in water with large bills always pointed toward the water, as if they're too heavy to lift. Feeds primarily by filtering tiny plants and insects from the water's surface with bill.

female

male pg. 229

SUMMER

GADWALL
Anas strepera

Size: 20" (50 cm)

Female: Very similar to the female Mallard. Mottled brown with pronounced color change from dark brown body to light brown neck and head. Wing linings are bright white, seen in flight. Small white wing patch, seen when swimming. Gray bill with orange sides.

Male: plump gray duck with a brown head and distinctive black rump, white belly, bright white wing linings, small white wing patch, chestnut-tinged wings, gray bill

Juvenile: similar to female

Nest: ground; female lines the nest with fine grass and down feathers plucked from her chest; 1 brood per year

Eggs: 8-11; white without markings

Incubation: 24-27 days; female incubates

Fledging: 48-56 days; young feed themselves

Migration: complete, to southern states and Mexico

Food: aquatic insects

Compare: The female Gadwall is very similar to female Mallard (pg. 181). Look for Gadwall's white wing patch and gray bill with orange sides.

Stan's Notes: A duck of shallow marshes. Consumes mostly plant material, dunking its head in water to feed rather than tipping forward, like other dabbling ducks. Walks well on land; feeds in fields and woodlands. Nests within 300 feet (100 m) of water. Often in pairs with other duck species. Establishes pair bond during winter.

soaring light
morph

intermediate
morph

light morph

dark morph

soaring dark
morph

SWAINSON'S HAWK
Buteo swainsoni

SUMMER

Size: 21" (53 cm); up to 4½-foot wingspan

Male: Highly variable-plumaged hawk with three easily distinguishable color morphs. Light morph is brown with a white belly, a warm rusty breast and a white face. Intermediate has a dark breast, rusty belly and white at the base of the bill. Dark morph is nearly all dark brown with a rusty color low on belly.

Female: same as male

Juvenile: similar to adult

Nest: platform; female and male build; 1 brood per year

Eggs: 2-4; bluish or white, some brown markings

Incubation: 28-35 days; female and male incubate

Fledging: 28-30 days; female and male feed young

Migration: complete, to Central and South America

Food: small mammals, insects, snakes, birds

Compare: Slimmer than the Red-tailed (pg. 171) with longer, more pointed wings and longer tail. Red-tailed has a white breast and a brown belly band. Ferruginous Hawk (pg. 175) lacks two-toned undersides of wings.

Stan's Notes: A slender open country hawk that hunts mammals, insects, snakes and birds when soaring (kiting) or perching. Often flies with slightly upturned wings in a teetering, vulture-like flight. The light morph is the most common of the three color types, with intermediate and dark also common. Even minor nest disturbance can cause nest failure. Often gathers in large flocks to migrate.

soaring

YEAR-ROUND
SUMMER

Size: 19-23" (48-58 cm); up to 4-foot wingspan

Male: Large hawk with amazing variety of colors from bird to bird, from chocolate brown to nearly all white. Often brown with a white breast and a distinctive brown belly band. Rust red tail usually only seen from above. Underside of wing is white with small dark patch on leading edge near shoulder.

Female: same as male, only slightly larger

Juvenile: similar to adults, lacking the red tail, has a speckled chest and light eyes

Nest: platform; male and female build; 1 brood per year

Eggs: 2-3; white without markings or sometimes marked with brown

Incubation: 30-35 days; female and male incubate

Fledging: 45-46 days; male and female feed young

Migration: non-migrator to partial migrator

Food: mice, birds, snakes, insects, mammals

Compare: Swainson's Hawk (pg. 169) is slimmer with longer, more pointed wings and longer tail.

Stan's Notes: A common hawk of open country and in cities in the Dakotas, frequently seen perched on freeway light posts, fences and trees. Look for it circling over open fields and roadsides, searching for prey. Their large stick nests are commonly seen in large trees along roads. Nests are lined with finer material such as evergreen tree needles. Will return to the same nest site each year. Doesn't develop red tail until the second year.

171

GREAT HORNED OWL
Bubo virginianus

Size: 20-25" (50-63 cm); up to 3½-foot wingspan

Male: Robust brown "horned" owl. Bright yellow eyes and V-shaped white throat resembling a necklace. Horizontal barring on the chest.

Female: same as male, only slightly larger

Juvenile: similar to adults, lacking ear tufts

Nest: no nest; takes over the nests of crows, Great Blue Herons and hawks, or will use partial cavities, stumps or broken-off trees; 1 brood per year

Eggs: 2; white without markings

Incubation: 26-30 days; female incubates

Fledging: 30-35 days; male and female feed young

Migration: non-migrator

Food: mammals, birds (ducks), snakes, insects

Compare: Burrowing Owl (pg. 131) is much smaller, has long legs and lacks feather tuft "horns." Great Horned Owl is over twice the size of Eastern Screech-Owl (pg. 213).

Stan's Notes: One of the earliest nesters in the Dakotas, laying eggs in January and February. It has excellent hearing; is able to hear a mouse moving beneath a foot of snow. "Ears" are actually tufts of feathers (horns) and have nothing to do with hearing. Not able to turn its head all the way around. Wing feathers are ragged on ends, resulting in a silent flight. The eyelids close from the top down, like humans. Fearless, it is one of the few animals that will kill skunks and porcupines. Because of this, it is sometimes called Flying Tiger.

soaring

soaring
juvenile

juvenile

FERRUGINOUS HAWK
Buteo regalis

YEAR-ROUND
MIGRATION
SUMMER

Size: 23" (58 cm); up to 4½-foot wingspan

Male: Pale brown head, gray cheeks, reddish back and white chin, chest and belly. Rust flanks extend down feathered legs. Bright white undersides of wings, light rust wing linings. Tail white below, rust-tinged on top. Large, strong yellow feet. Red eyes. Dark eye line.

Female: same as male, but noticeably larger

Juvenile: brown head, nape, back and wings with a white chin, chest and belly

Nest: massive platform, low in a tree, sometimes on the ground; female and male build; 1 brood per year

Eggs: 2-4; bluish or white, can have brown marks

Incubation: 28-33 days; female and male incubate

Fledging: 44-48 days; female and male feed young

Migration: complete, to southern states and Mexico

Food: larger mammals, snakes, insects, birds

Compare: The Swainson's Hawk (pg. 169) is smaller and has two-toned undersides of wings. The Red-tailed Hawk (pg. 171) has a brown belly band and lacks rust flanks and legs.

Stan's Notes: The largest hawk species. Found in western prairies. Common name means "iron-like," referring to the rusty color. Male and female perform an aerial courtship, soaring with wings held above their backs, male diving at female, grabbing at each other with large, powerful feet. Often hunts larger mammals such as jack rabbits. Often stands on the ground. Nests in most of the Dakotas.

male pg. 231

female

NORTHERN HARRIER
Circus cyaneus

YEAR-ROUND
SUMMER

Size: 23" (58 cm); up to 3½-foot wingspan

Female: A slim, low-flying hawk. Dark brown back with brown-streaked breast and belly. Large white rump patch and narrow black bands across tail. Tips of wings black. Yellow eyes.

Male: silver gray with large white rump patch and white belly, faint narrow bands across tail, tips of wings black, yellow eyes

Juvenile: similar to female, with an orange breast

Nest: platform, often on ground; female and male build; 1 brood per year

Eggs: 4-8; bluish white without markings

Incubation: 31-32 days; female incubates

Fledging: 30-35 days; male and female feed young

Migration: partial, to southern states, Mexico, Central America, non-migrator in South Dakota

Food: mice, snakes, insects, small birds

Compare: Slimmer than Red-tailed Hawk (pg. 171). Look for black bands on tail and a white rump patch.

Stan's Notes: One of the easiest hawks to identify. Harriers glide just above ground, following contours of the land while searching for prey. Holds its wings just above the horizontal position, tilting back and forth in the wind, similar to Turkey Vultures. Formerly called Marsh Hawk due to its habit of hunting over marshes. Feeds on the ground. Will perch on the ground to preen and rest. At any age, has a distinctive owl-like face disk.

NORTHERN PINTAIL
Anas acuta

SUMMER

Size:	26" (66 cm), male 21" (53 cm), female
Male:	A slender, elegant duck with a brown head, white neck, gray body and extremely long, narrow black tail. Gray bill. Non-breeding has a pale brown head that lacks the clear demarcation between the brown head and white neck. Lacks long tail feathers.
Female:	mottled brown body with a paler head and neck, long tail, gray bill
Juvenile:	similar to female
Nest:	ground; female builds; 1 brood per year
Eggs:	6-9; olive green without markings
Incubation:	22-25 days; female incubates
Fledging:	36-50 days; female teaches young to feed
Migration:	partial, to southern states and Mexico
Food:	aquatic plants and insects, seeds
Compare:	The male Northern Pintail has a distinctive brown head and white neck. Look for the unique long tail feathers. The female Pintail is similar to female Mallard (pg. 181), but Mallard has an orange bill with black spots.

Stan's Notes: A common dabbling duck of alkaline marshes. Tips forward to reach food on marsh or pond bottom. Diet is about 90 percent aquatic plants, except when females feed heavily on insects prior to nesting, gaining extra nutrients for egg production. Male molts in winter, appearing more like female. Flies in line formation.

male pg. 245

female

YEAR-ROUND
SUMMER

MALLARD
Anas platyrhynchos

Size: 27-28" (69-71 cm)

Female: All brown with orange and black bill. Small blue and white wing mark (speculum).

Male: large, bulbous green head, white necklace, rust brown or chestnut chest, combination of gray and white on the sides, yellow bill, orange legs and feet

Juvenile: same as female, but with a yellow bill

Nest: ground; female builds; 1 brood per year

Eggs: 7-10; greenish to whitish, unmarked

Incubation: 26-30 days; female incubates

Fledging: 42-52 days; female leads young to food

Migration: non-migrator to partial in the Dakotas

Food: seeds, plants, aquatic insects; will come to ground feeders offering corn

Compare: Female Gadwall (pg. 167) has a gray bill with orange sides. The female Wood Duck (pg. 161) is smaller, with a white eye-ring. Female Northern Shoveler (pg. 165) has a large spoon-shaped bill. Female Northern Pintail (pg. 179) is similar, with a gray bill.

Stan's Notes: A familiar duck of lakes and ponds, it's considered a type of dabbling duck, tipping forward in shallow water to feed on aquatic plants on the bottom. The name "Mallard" comes from the Latin *masculus*, meaning "male," referring to the habit of males not taking part in raising ducklings. Both female and male have white tails and white underwings. Black central tail feathers of male curl upward. Will return to place of birth.

181

AMERICAN BITTERN
Botaurus lentiginosus

Size: 28" (71 cm)

Male: Overall brown with thick rusty striping on neck, chest and belly. White chin. A unique shape with an extremely long neck, round compact body and short tail. Green legs and feet. Long, pointed yellow bill. Golden eyes.

Female: same as male

Juvenile: similar to adult

Nest: ground; female builds; 1 brood per year

Eggs: 4-5; light brown without markings

Incubation: 28-29 days; female incubates

Fledging: 7-14 days; male and female teach young what to eat

Migration: complete, to southern coastal states, Mexico

Food: small fish, aquatic insects, amphibians

Compare: The Black-crowned Night-Heron (pg. 49) is gray and white with a black cap and dark bill. Great Blue Heron (pg. 237) is much larger and has grayish blue plumage.

Stan's Notes: Very secretive bird that seems to be on the decline. Hunts by walking extremely slowly, looking for prey along edges of ponds, streams and wetlands. Strikes an erect posture and points its large yellow bill straight up into the air to disguise itself. Carries this camouflage one step further, swaying back and forth in wind to match surrounding cattails and other aquatic vegetation (reeds). Strikes quickly at prey with its sharp bill. Usually solitary, roosting in trees at any hour. The male's loud booming call sounds like a slow water pump, hence its other common name, Slue-pumper.

GREATER WHITE-FRONTED GOOSE
Anser albifrons

Size: 28" (71 cm)

Male: Grayish brown with distinctive white band at the base of bill. Irregular black barring on breast and belly. Bill is light pink to orange, often with a white tip. Orange legs and feet. White rump and undertail.

Female: same as male

Juvenile: lighter color than adult, with yellowish bill, legs and feet

Nest: ground; female builds; 1 brood per year

Eggs: 4-7; creamy white without markings

Incubation: 23-25 days; female incubates

Fledging: 40-45 days; male and female teach young to feed

Migration: complete, to coastal Texas and Mexico

Food: aquatic plants and insects

Compare: Similar size as the Snow Goose (pg. 267). White morph Snow Goose is all white with black wing tips and a large bright pink bill. The blue morph Snow Goose usually has a white head and dark gray body.

Stan's Notes: Over half of the North American population (over 1 million birds) migrate through the Dakotas. Hybridizes with Snow and Canada Geese; often seen with them in mixed flocks or flying high up in large wedge shapes. Learns migratory route from parents and older members of flock. Doesn't breed until 3 years of age. Nests in Canadian Northwest Territories and Alaska. Often called Speckled-bellied by hunters due to the irregular marking on belly.

YEAR-ROUND

RING-NECKED PHEASANT
Phasianus colchicus

Size: 30-36" (76-90 cm), male, including tail
21-25" (53-63 cm), female, including tail

Male: Golden brown body with a long tail. White ring around neck with purple, green, blue and red head.

Female: smaller, less flamboyant all-brown bird with a long tail

Juvenile: similar to female, with a shorter tail

Nest: ground; female builds; 1 brood per year

Eggs: 8-10; olive brown without markings

Incubation: 23-25 days; female incubates

Fledging: 11-12 days; female leads young to food

Migration: non-migrator

Food: insects, seeds, fruit; visits ground feeders

Compare: Male and female Pheasants have long tails, but the male is brightly colored.

Stan's Notes: Introduced from China in the late 1800s. Common now across the U.S., and widespread and abundant in the Dakotas. Their numbers vary greatly, however, making them common in some years and scarce in others, like many other game birds. The name "Ring-necked" refers to the thin white ring around the male's neck. The name "Pheasant" comes from the Greek word *phaisianos*, meaning "bird of the River Phasis." (The Phasis, located in Europe, is now known as the River Rioni.) Listen for the male's cackling call to attract females.

YEAR-ROUND

WILD TURKEY
Meleagris gallopavo

Size: 36-48" (90-120 cm)

Male: Large, plump brown and bronze bird with striking blue and red bare head. Fan tail and long, straight black beard in center of chest. Spurs on legs.

Female: thinner and less striking than male, usually lacking breast beard

Juvenile: same as adult of the same sex

Nest: ground; female builds; 1 brood per year

Eggs: 10-12; buff white with dull brown markings

Incubation: 27-28 days; female incubates

Fledging: 6-10 days; female leads young to food

Migration: non-migrator

Food: insects, seeds, fruit

Compare: This bird is quite distinctive and unlikely to be confused with others.

Stan's Notes: The largest game bird in the Dakotas, and the bird from which the domestic turkey was bred. Almost became our national bird, losing to the Bald Eagle by just one vote. Strong fliers, they can approach 60 miles (97 km) per hour. Able to fly straight up, then away. Eyesight is three times better than human eyesight. Hearing is also excellent; can hear competing males up to a mile away. Males hold "harems" of up to 20 females. Males are known as toms, females are hens and young are poults. At night, they roost in trees.

RUBY-CROWNED KINGLET
Regulus calendula

MIGRATION
SUMMER

Size: 4" (10 cm)

Male: Small, teardrop-shaped green-to-gray bird. Two white wing bars. Hidden ruby-colored crown. White eye-ring.

Female: same as male, but lacking the ruby crown

Juvenile: same as female

Nest: pendulous; female builds; 1 brood per year

Eggs: 4-5; white with brown markings

Incubation: 11-12 days; female incubates

Fledging: 11-12 days; female and male feed young

Migration: complete, to southern states, Mexico and Central America

Food: insects, berries

Compare: The female American Goldfinch (pg. 277) is larger, but shares the same olive color and unmarked breast. Look for the white eye-ring of Ruby-crowned Kinglet.

Stan's Notes: One of the smaller birds in the Dakotas, it takes a quick eye to see the male's ruby crown. Usually seen only during migration, except in the Black Hills of South Dakota. Look for it flitting around thick shrubs low to the ground. Builds an unusual pendulous (sac-like) nest, intricately woven and decorated on the outside with colored lichens and mosses stuck together with spider webs. Nest is suspended from a branch overlapped by leaves and usually is hung high in a mature tree. Common name "Kinglet" comes from the Anglo-Saxon word *cyning*, or "king," referring to the male's ruby crown, and diminutive suffix "let," meaning "small."

RED-BREASTED NUTHATCH
Sitta canadensis

Size: 4½" (11 cm)

Male: A small gray-backed bird with a black cap and a prominent eye line. A rust red breast and belly.

Female: gray cap, pale undersides

Juvenile: same as female

Nest: cavity; female builds; 1 brood per year

Eggs: 5-6; white with red brown markings

Incubation: 11-12 days; female incubates

Fledging: 14-20 days; female and male feed young

Migration: irruptive; moves around North and South Dakota in search of food

Food: insects, seeds; visits seed and suet feeders

Compare: Smaller than the White-breasted Nuthatch (pg. 197), with a red chest instead of white.

Stan's Notes: The Red-breasted Nuthatch behaves like the White-breasted Nuthatch, climbing down tree trunks headfirst. Similar to chickadees, visits seed feeders, quickly grabbing a seed and flying off to crack it open. Will wedge a seed into a crevice and pound it open with several sharp blows. The name "Nuthatch" comes from the Middle English moniker *nuthak*, referring to the bird's habit of wedging a seed into a crevice and hacking it open. Look for it in mature conifers, where it often extracts seeds from cones. Doesn't excavate a cavity as a chickadee might; rather, it takes over an old woodpecker or chickadee cavity. A winter visitor and a year-round resident in some parts of North and South Dakota. More abundant in some years and absent in others.

BLACK-CAPPED CHICKADEE
Poecile atricapillus

YEAR-ROUND

Size: 5" (13 cm)

Male: Familiar gray bird with black cap and throat patch. White chest. Tan belly. Small white wing marks.

Female: same as male

Juvenile: same as adult

Nest: cavity; female and male build or excavate; 1 brood per year

Eggs: 5-7; white with fine brown markings

Incubation: 11-13 days; female and male incubate

Fledging: 14-18 days; female and male feed young

Migration: non-migrator

Food: insects, seeds, fruit; comes to seed and suet feeders

Compare: A familiar backyard bird whose energy and friendliness is hard to mistake.

Stan's Notes: Widespread, common bird throughout the Dakotas. It is a backyard bird that can be attracted with a simple nest box or seed feeder. Usually is the first to find a new feeder. Can be easily tamed and hand fed. Can be a common urban bird since much of its diet comes from bird feeders. Needs to feed each day in winter; consequently seen foraging for food during even the worst winter storms. Frequently seen with other birds such as nuthatches and woodpeckers. Makes its nest mostly with green moss, lining it with animal fur. Common name comes from its familiar "chika-dee-dee-dee-dee" call. It also gives a high-pitched, two-toned "fee-bee" call. Can have different calls in various regions.

WHITE-BREASTED NUTHATCH
Sitta carolinensis

YEAR-ROUND

Size: 5-6" (13-15 cm)

Male: Slate gray with a white face and belly, and black cap and nape. Long thin bill, slightly upturned. Chestnut undertail.

Female: similar to male, gray cap and nape

Juvenile: similar to female

Nest: cavity; the female and male build; 1 brood per year

Eggs: 5-7; white with brown markings

Incubation: 11-12 days; female incubates

Fledging: 13-14 days; female and male feed young

Migration: non-migrator

Food: insects, seeds; visits seed and suet feeders

Compare: Red-breasted Nuthatch (pg. 193) is smaller, with a rust red belly and a distinctive black eye line.

Stan's Notes: The nuthatch's habit of hopping headfirst down tree trunks helps it see insects and insect eggs that birds climbing up the trunk might miss. Incredible climbing agility comes from an extra-long hind toe claw or nail, nearly twice the size of the front toe claws. The name "Nuthatch" comes from the Middle English moniker *nuthak*, referring to the bird's habit of wedging a seed into a crevice and hacking it open. Frequently seen in mixed flocks of chickadees and Downy Woodpeckers. Will use a nest box. Mated pairs remain together all year, defending small territories. Listen for its characteristic spring call, "whi-whi-whi-whi," given in February and March. One of 17 worldwide nuthatch species.

male

female

YELLOW-RUMPED WARBLER
Dendroica coronata

Size: 5-6" (13-15 cm)

Male: Slate gray bird with black streaks on breast. Yellow patch on the head, flanks and rump. White chin and belly. Two white wing bars.

Female: duller than male, but same yellow patches

Juvenile: similar to female

Nest: cup; female builds; 2 broods per year

Eggs: 4-5; white with brown markings

Incubation: 12-13 days; female incubates

Fledging: 10-12 days; female and male feed young

Migration: complete, to southern states, Mexico and Central America

Food: insects, berries; rarely comes to suet feeders

Compare: The Common Yellowthroat (pg. 279) has a yellow breast, unlike the Yellow-rumped's patches of yellow. The male Yellow Warbler (pg. 283) is all yellow with orange streaks on breast. Look for a combination of yellow patches on the head, flanks and rump.

Stan's Notes: A common migrating warbler and summer resident in parts of the Dakotas. Flocks of hundreds seen during migration, usually arriving in late September to early October. Builds nest in coniferous and aspen forests. Male molts to a dull color in winter similar to female, retaining the yellow patches. Sometimes called Butter-butts due to the yellow patch on rump. Was formerly called Audubon's or Myrtle Warbler. Familiar call is a robust "chip."

female
pg. 83

male

DARK-EYED JUNCO
Junco hyemalis

WINTER

Size: 5½" (14 cm)

Male: A round, dark-eyed bird with slate-gray-to-charcoal chest, head and back. White belly. Pink bill. Since the outermost tail feathers are white, tail appears as a white V in flight.

Female: same as male, only tan-to-brown color

Juvenile: similar to female, but has a streaked breast and head

Nest: cup; female and male build; 2 broods a year

Eggs: 3-5; white with reddish brown markings

Incubation: 12-13 days; female incubates

Fledging: 10-13 days; male and female feed young

Migration: complete, throughout the U.S.; winters in the Dakotas

Food: seeds, insects; will come to seed feeders

Compare: Rarely confused with any other bird. Small flocks feed under bird feeders in winter.

Stan's Notes: Common in winter, this bird is usually seen on the ground in small flocks. It adheres to a rigid social hierarchy, with dominant birds chasing less dominant birds. Look for white outer tail feathers flashing while it is in flight. Most comfortable on the ground, juncos will "double-scratch" with both feet to expose seeds and insects. Consumes many weed seeds. Several junco species have now been combined into one, simply called Dark-eyed Junco. Doesn't nest in the Dakotas.

EASTERN PHOEBE
Sayornis phoebe

Size: 7" (18 cm)

Male: Gray bird with dark wings, light olive green belly and a thin dark bill.

Female: same as male

Juvenile: same as adult

Nest: cup; female builds; 2 broods per year

Eggs: 4-5; white without markings

Incubation: 15-16 days; female incubates

Fledging: 15-16 days; male and female feed young

Migration: complete, to southern states and Mexico

Food: insects

Compare: Like most other olive gray birds, it is hard to distinguish identifying markings. Eastern Phoebe lacks any white eye-ring. Easier to identify by well-enunciated song, "fee-bee," or characteristic of hawking for insects.

Stan's Notes: A sparrow-sized bird often seen on the end of a dead branch. It sits in wait for a passing insect, flies out to catch it, then returns to the same branch, a process called hawking. Has a habit of pumping its tail up and down and spreading it when perched. Will build its nest under the eaves of a house, under a bridge or in culverts. Nest is constructed with mud, grass and moss, and lined with hair (and sometimes feathers). The name is derived from its characteristic song, "fee-bee," which is repeated over and over from the tops of dead branches.

GREAT CRESTED FLYCATCHER
Myiarchus crinitus

Size: 8" (20 cm)

Male: Gray head with prominent crest. Gray back and throat with bright yellow belly, yellow extending under reddish brown tail. Lower bill is yellow at base.

Female: same as male

Juvenile: same as adult

Nest: cavity; the female and male build; 1 brood per year

Eggs: 4-6; white or buff with brown markings

Incubation: 13-15 days; female incubates

Fledging: 14-21 days; female and male feed young

Migration: complete, to Mexico and Central America

Food: insects, fruit

Compare: The Eastern Kingbird (pg. 207) has a white band across the tail. Similar to the Eastern Phoebe (pg. 203), but the Flycatcher has an obvious crest and yellow belly.

Stan's Notes: Common bird of wooded areas in North and South Dakota. It lives high up in the trees, rarely coming to the ground. Often heard before seen. The first part of its common name refers to the set of extra long feathers on the top of its head (crest), which the bird raises when alert or agitated, similar to Northern Cardinals. Feeds by gleaning insects from tree leaves. Nests in old woodpecker holes, but can be attracted to a nest box placed high in a tree with a 1½- to 2½-inch (4 to 6 cm) entrance hole. Often stuffs its nest with a collection of fur, feathers, string and snakeskins.

EASTERN KINGBIRD
Tyrannus tyrannus

Size: 8" (20 cm)

Male: Mostly black gray bird with white belly and chin. Black head and tail with a distinctive white band across the end of the tail. Has a concealed red crown that is rarely seen.

Female: same as male

Juvenile: same as adult

Nest: cup; male and female build; 1 brood a year

Eggs: 3-4; white with brown markings

Incubation: 16-18 days; female incubates

Fledging: 16-18 days; female and male feed young

Migration: complete, to Mexico, Central America and South America

Food: insects, fruit

Compare: Rarely confused with other birds. Lacks any yellow of the Western Kingbird (pg. 295). Medium-sized bird, smaller than American Robin (pg. 217). Look for the white band along the end of the tail to identify.

Stan's Notes: Common bird throughout the Dakotas in open fields and prairies. Autumn migration begins in late August and early September, with groups of up to 20 individuals migrating together. Returns to mating ground in spring, where male and female defend their territory. Acting unafraid of other birds and chasing the larger ones, it is perceived as having an attitude. Bold behavior gave rise to the common name, King. Perches on tall branches, watching for insects. After flying out to catch them, returns to the same perch, a technique called hawking.

GRAY CATBIRD
Dumetella carolinensis

Size: 9" (22.5 cm)

Male: Handsome slate gray bird with black crown and a long, thin black bill. Often seen with its tail lifted, exposing a chestnut-colored patch under tail.

Female: same as male

Juvenile: same as adult

Nest: cup; female and male build; 2 broods a year

Eggs: 4-6; blue green without markings

Incubation: 12-13 days; female incubates

Fledging: 10-11 days; female and male feed young

Migration: complete, to southern states

Food: insects, fruit

Compare: Larger than Eastern Phoebe (pg. 203), it lacks the Phoebe's olive belly. Similar size as Eastern Kingbird (pg. 207), but it lacks the Kingbird's white belly and white tail band.

Stan's Notes: Returns to North and South Dakota by the last week of April. Seen in great numbers during fall migration in the last week of September and in early October. A secretive bird that the Chippewa Indians named Bird That Cries With Grief due to its raspy call. The call sounds like the mewing of a house cat, hence the common name. Often mimics other birds, rarely repeating the same phrases. More frequently heard than seen. Nests only in thick shrubs, and quickly flies back into shrubs when approached. If a cowbird introduces an egg into a catbird nest, the catbird quickly break its, then ejects it.

LOGGERHEAD SHRIKE
Lanius ludovicianus

Size: 9" (22.5 cm)

Male: A gray head and back with black wings and mask across the eyes. A white chin, breast and belly. Black tail, legs and feet. Black bill with hooked tip. White wing patches, seen in flight.

Female: same as male

Juvenile: dull version of adult

Nest: cup; the male and female build; 1-2 broods per year

Eggs: 4-7; off-white with dark markings

Incubation: 16-17 days; female incubates

Fledging: 17-21 days; female and male feed young

Migration: complete, to southern states and Mexico

Food: insects, lizards, small mammals, frogs

Compare: Distinctive-looking bird. Look for the black wings and mask across the eyes to help identify. Cedar Waxwing (pg. 115) also has a black mask, but is brown, not gray and black like the Shrike.

Stan's Notes: The Loggerhead is a songbird that acts like a bird of prey. Known for skewering prey on barbed wire fences, thorns and other sharp objects to store or hold still while tearing apart to eat, hence its other common name, Butcher Bird. Feet are too weak to hold the prey it eats. Breeding bird surveys indicate declining populations in the Great Plains due to pesticides killing its major food source–grasshoppers.

red morph

gray morph

EASTERN SCREECH-OWL
Megascops asio

Size: 9" (22.5 cm); up to 20-inch wingspan

Male: Small "eared" owl that occurs in one of two permanent color morphs. Is either mottled with gray and white, or is red brown (rust) with white. Bright yellow eyes.

Female: same as male

Juvenile: lighter color than adult of the same morph, usually no ear tufts

Nest: cavity, former woodpecker cavity; does not add any nesting material; 1 brood per year

Eggs: 4-5; white without markings

Incubation: 25-26 days; female incubates, male feeds female during incubation

Fledging: 26-27 days; male and female feed young

Migration: non-migrator

Food: large insects, small mammals, birds, snakes

Compare: The only small owl in the Dakotas that has ear tufts. Can be gray or rust-colored.

Stan's Notes: A common owl active at dusk and during the night. Excellent hearing and eyesight. Will seldom give a screeching call; more commonly gives a tremulous, descending whiny trill, like a sound effect of a scary movie. Will nest in a wooden nest box. Often seen sunning themselves at nest box holes during the winter. Male and female may roost together at night, and are thought to mate for life. Different colorations are known as morphs. The gray morph is more common than the red.

213

SUMMER

WILSON'S PHALAROPE
Phalaropus tricolor

Size: 9¼" (23 cm)

Female: An overall gray bird with a black stripe that runs from the base of bill across eyes and down the neck. Rusty wash on the front of neck. White chin and sides of body. Long black legs. Thin black bill.

Male: similar to female, but duller

Juvenile: similar to male, but has yellow legs

Nest: ground; male builds; 1-2 broods per year

Eggs: 3-4; pale white, brown and black markings

Incubation: 16-21 days; male incubates

Fledging: 8-10 days; male teaches young what to eat

Migration: complete, to South America

Food: small aquatic insects, seeds

Compare: Upland Sandpiper (pg. 147) has a yellow bill. Breeding Spotted Sandpiper (pg. 121) has a speckled white chest and belly. Lesser Yellowlegs (pg. 135) lacks the female's neck stripe. Look for it swimming in tight circles.

Stan's Notes: Unique shorebird, one of the few that swims. Female is often larger and more colorful than male. Female abandons male after laying eggs. Male cares for young. Often swims in tight circles, creating a whirlpool effect that raises insects to the surface. Picks insects off the water. Unlike other shorebirds, has lobed toes. Often seen alone or in small groups. Often feeds with American Avocets in shallow water. One of three phalarope species in North America and the only one that breeds south of Canada and Alaska. Breeding season from April to August.

AMERICAN ROBIN
Turdus migratorius

Size: 9-11" (22.5-28 cm)

Male: A familiar gray bird with a rusty red breast, and nearly black head and tail. White chin with black streaks. White eye-ring.

Female: similar to male, but with a gray head and a duller breast

Juvenile: similar to female, but has a speckled breast and brown back

Nest: cup; female builds with help from the male; 2-3 broods per year

Eggs: 4-7; pale blue without markings

Incubation: 12-14 days; female incubates

Fledging: 14-16 days; female and male feed young

Migration: complete, to southern states, Mexico and Central America, non-migrator in South Dakota and southern half of North Dakota

Food: insects, fruit, berries, worms

Compare: Familiar bird to all.

Stan's Notes: Although complete migrators in northern states, the robin is a year-round resident in the southern half of North Dakota and throughout South Dakota. Can be heard singing all night long in spring. Most people don't realize how easy it is to differentiate between male and female robins. Compare the male's dark, nearly black head and brick red breast with the female's gray head and dull red breast. Robins are not listening for worms when they cock their heads to one side. They are looking with eyes that are placed far back on the sides of their heads. A very territorial bird. Often seen fighting its own reflection in windows.

soaring

juvenile

SHARP-SHINNED HAWK
Accipiter striatus

YEAR-ROUND
MIGRATION
SUMMER
WINTER

Size: 10-14" (25-36 cm); up to 2-foot wingspan

Male: Small woodland hawk with gray back and head, and rusty red breast. Long tail with several dark tail bands, widest band at end of squared-off tail. Red eyes.

Female: same as male, only larger

Juvenile: same size as adults, with a brown back and heavily streaked breast, yellow eyes

Nest: platform; female builds; 1 brood per year

Eggs: 4-5; white with brown markings

Incubation: 32-35 days; female incubates

Fledging: 24-27 days; female and male feed young

Migration: complete, southern states, Mexico, Central America; winters in parts of South Dakota

Food: birds, small mammals

Compare: Nearly identical to Cooper's Hawk (pg. 227), only smaller. Look for the Sharp-shinned's squared tail, compared with the rounded tail of the Cooper's.

Stan's Notes: A common hawk of backyards and woodlands, often seen swooping in on birds visiting feeders. Its short rounded wings and long tail allow this hawk to navigate through thick stands of trees in pursuit of prey. Common name comes from the sharp keel on the leading edge of its "shin," though it is actually below rather than above the bird's ankle on the tarsus bone of foot. The tarsus in most birds is round. In flight, head doesn't protrude as far as the head of the Cooper's Hawk.

ROCK PIGEON
Columba livia

Size: 13" (33 cm)

Male: No set color pattern. Gray to white, patches of iridescent greens and blues, usually with a light rump patch.

Female: same as male

Juvenile: same as adult

Nest: platform; female builds; 3-4 broods a year

Eggs: 1-2; white without markings

Incubation: 18-20 days; female and male incubate

Fledging: 25-26 days; female and male feed young

Migration: non-migrator

Food: seeds

Compare: The Mourning Dove (pg. 145) is smaller and light brown in color.

Stan's Notes: Also known as Domestic Pigeon, it was introduced to North America from Europe by the early settlers. Most common around cities and barnyards, where it scratches for seeds. One of the few birds that has a wide variety of colors, produced by years of selective breeding while in captivity. Parents feed their young a regurgitated liquid known as crop-milk for the first few days of life. One of the few birds that can drink without tilting its head back. Nests under bridges and on buildings, balconies, barns and sheds. Was once poisoned as a "nuisance city bird." Many cities now have Peregrine Falcons (not shown) that feed on Rock Pigeons, keeping their numbers in check.

winter

breeding

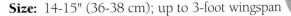

FRANKLIN'S GULL
Larus pipixcan

MIGRATION
SUMMER

Size: 14-15" (36-38 cm); up to 3-foot wingspan

Male: Gray and white plumage with a black head, black extending partially down the neck and black wing tips. Large white eye-ring. Reddish bill. Winter plumage has a partial black "hood" and black bill.

Female: same as male

Juvenile: brown back, black bill, lacks all-black head

Nest: floating platform; male and female build; 1 brood per year

Eggs: 2-4; greenish with brown markings

Incubation: 24-25 days; female and male incubate

Fledging: 31-33 days; female and male feed young

Migration: complete, to southern states, Mexico, and Central and South America

Food: insects, fish

Compare: The only black-headed gull in the Dakotas during summer and migration. Look for it in open marshes, with its black "hood" and black wing tips.

Stan's Notes: Usually seen during spring and fall migrations, when hundreds gather in prairie lakes and reservoirs. A three-year gull, young obtain adult plumage at 3 years of age. Juveniles are brown with partially black heads. The first- and second-year birds are like winter adults, with gray and white plumage, partially black heads and black bills. Winters on the Pacific coast, all along Central and South America. Breeding range is from South Dakota to western Iowa and Minnesota to across Canada.

breeding
pg. 151

displaying

winter

WILLET
Catoptrophorus semipalmatus

MIGRATION
SUMMER

Size: 15" (38 cm)

Male: Winter plumage is gray with a gray bill and legs. White belly. A distinctive black and white wing lining pattern, seen in flight or during display.

Female: same as male

Juvenile: similar to breeding adult, more tan in color

Nest: ground; female builds; 1 brood per year

Eggs: 3-5; olive green with dark markings

Incubation: 24-28 days; male and female incubate

Fledging: unknown days; female and male feed young

Migration: complete, to southern coastal states, coastal Central and South America

Food: aquatic insects

Compare: Larger than the Lesser Yellowlegs (pg. 135), which has yellow legs.

Stan's Notes: Common summer resident in the Dakotas, also seen during migration. Appearing a rich, warm brown during breeding season and rather plain gray in winter, it always has a striking black and white wing pattern when seen flying. Uses its black and white wing patches to display to mate. Named after the "pill-will-willet" call it gives during the breeding season. Gives a "kip-kip-kip" alarm call when it takes flight. Also nests in other western states, along the East coast and in Canada.

225

soaring

juvenile

COOPER'S HAWK
Accipiter cooperii

Size: 14-20" (36-50 cm); up to 2½-foot wingspan

Male: Medium-sized hawk with short wings and long rounded tail with several black bands. Rusty breast and dark wing tips. Slate gray back. Bright yellow spot at base of gray bill (cere). Dark red eyes.

Female: similar to male, only slightly larger

Juvenile: brown back with brown streaks on breast, bright yellow eyes

Nest: platform; male and female build; 1 brood per year

Eggs: 2-4; greenish with brown markings

Incubation: 32-36 days; female and male incubate

Fledging: 28-32 days; male and female feed young

Migration: complete, to southern states and Mexico, non-migrator in South Dakota

Food: small birds, mammals

Compare: Nearly identical to the Sharp-shinned Hawk (pg. 219), only larger, darker gray and with a rounded-off tail.

Stan's Notes: Resident hawk in Dakota woodlands. In flight, look for its large head, short wings and long tail. The short stubby wings help it maneuver between trees while pursuing small birds. Will come to feeders, hunting for unaware birds. Flies with long glides followed by a few quick flaps. Known to ambush prey, it will fly into heavy brush or even run on the ground in pursuit. Nestlings have gray eyes that become bright yellow at 1 year of age and dark red later.

female pg. 167

male

SUMMER

GADWALL
Anas strepera

Size: 20" (50 cm)

Male: A plump gray duck with a brown head and a distinctive black rump. White belly and chestnut-tinged wings. Bright white wing linings. Small white wing patch, seen when swimming. Gray bill.

Female: similar to female Mallard, a mottled brown with a pronounced color change from dark brown body to light brown neck and head, bright white wing linings, small white wing patch, gray bill with orange sides

Juvenile: similar to female

Nest: ground; female lines the nest with fine grass and down feathers plucked from her chest; 1 brood per year

Eggs: 8-11; white without markings

Incubation: 24-27 days; female incubates

Fledging: 48-56 days; young feed themselves

Migration: complete, to southern states and Mexico

Food: aquatic insects

Compare: Male Gadwall is one of the few gray-colored ducks. Look for its distinctive black rump.

Stan's Notes: A duck of shallow marshes. Consumes mostly plant material, dunking its head in water to feed rather than tipping forward, like other dabbling ducks. Walks well on land; feeds in fields and woodlands. Nests within 300 feet (100 m) of water. Often in pairs with other duck species. Establishes pair bond during winter.

male

female pg. 177

YEAR-ROUND
SUMMER

NORTHERN HARRIER
Circus cyaneus

Size: 23" (58 cm); up to 3½-foot wingspan

Male: A slim, low-flying hawk. Silver gray with a large white rump patch and a white belly. Faint narrow bands across the tail. Tips of wings black. Yellow eyes.

Female: dark brown back, a brown-streaked breast and belly, large white rump patch, narrow black bands across tail, tips of wings black, yellow eyes

Juvenile: similar to female, with an orange breast

Nest: platform, often on ground; female and male build; 1 brood per year

Eggs: 4-8; bluish white without markings

Incubation: 31-32 days; female incubates

Fledging: 30-35 days; male and female feed young

Migration: partial, to southern states, Mexico, Central America, non-migrator in South Dakota

Food: mice, snakes, insects, small birds

Compare: Slimmer than Red-tailed Hawk (pg. 171). Look for black bands on tail and a white rump patch.

Stan's Notes: One of the easiest hawks to identify. Harriers glide just above ground, following contours of the land while searching for prey. Holds its wings just above the horizontal position, tilting back and forth in the wind, similar to Turkey Vultures. Formerly called Marsh Hawk due to its habit of hunting over marshes. Feeds on the ground. Will perch on the ground to preen and rest. At any age, has a distinctive owl-like face disk.

CANADA GOOSE
Branta canadensis

Size: 25-43" (63-109 cm)

Male: Large gray goose with black neck and head, with a white chin or cheek strap.

Female: same as male

Juvenile: same as adult

Nest: platform, on the ground; female builds; 1 brood per year

Eggs: 5-10; white without markings

Incubation: 25-30 days; female incubates

Fledging: 42-55 days; male and female teach young to feed

Migration: non-migrator to partial migrator

Food: aquatic plants, insects, seeds

Compare: Large goose that is rarely confused with any other bird.

Stan's Notes: Breeds throughout North and South Dakota. Adults mate for many years, but only start to breed in the third year. Males often act as sentinels, standing at the edge of a group, bobbing their heads up and down, becoming very aggressive to anybody who approaches. Will hiss as if displaying displeasure. Adults molt primary flight feathers while raising young, rendering family groups flightless at the same time. Several subspecies vary geographically around the U.S. Generally they are paler in color in eastern groups and darker in western. Size decreases northward, with the smallest subspecies found on the Arctic tundra.

SANDHILL CRANE
Grus canadensis

MIGRATION
SUMMER

Size:	40-48" (102-120 cm); up to 7-foot wingspan
Male:	Elegant gray bird with long legs and neck. Wings and body often stained rusty brown. Scarlet red cap. Yellow-to-red eyes.
Female:	same as male
Juvenile:	dull brown, lacks red cap, has yellow eyes
Nest:	platform, on the ground; female and male build; 1 brood per year
Eggs:	2; olive with brown markings
Incubation:	28-32 days; female and male incubate
Fledging:	65 days; female and male feed young
Migration:	complete, to southern states and Mexico
Food:	insects, fruit, worms, plants, amphibians
Compare:	Similar size as Great Blue Heron (pg. 237), but the Crane has a shorter bill and red cap. Great Blue Heron flies with neck held in an S shape, unlike the Crane's straight neck.

Stan's Notes: Among the tallest birds in the world and capable of flying at great heights. Usually seen in large undisturbed fields near water. Often heard before seen, they have a very distinctive rattling call. Plumage often appears rust brown because of staining from mud during preening. Characteristic flight with upstroke quicker than down. For their spectacular mating dance the performers face each other, bow and jump into the air while uttering loud cackling sounds and flapping wings. Often flips sticks and grass into the air during dance.

GREAT BLUE HERON
Ardea herodias

Size: 42-52" (107-132 cm)

Male: Tall gray heron. Black eyebrows extend into several long plumes off the back of head. Long yellow bill. Feathers at base of neck drop down in a kind of necklace.

Female: same as male

Juvenile: same as adult, but more brown than gray, with a black crown and no plumes

Nest: platform; male and female build; 1 brood per year

Eggs: 3-5; blue green without markings

Incubation: 27-28 days; female and male incubate

Fledging: 56-60 days; male and female feed young

Migration: complete, to southern states, Mexico, and Central and South America

Food: small fish, frogs, insects, snakes

Compare: Similar size as the Sandhill Crane (pg. 235), but lacks the Crane's red crown. Crane flies with neck held straight, unlike the Heron's S-shaped neck.

Stan's Notes: One of the most common herons, often barking like a dog when startled. Seen stalking small fish in shallow water. Will strike at mice, squirrels and just about anything else it might come across. Flies holding neck in an S shape, with its long legs trailing straight out behind. The wings are held in cupped fashion during flight. Nests in colonies of up to 100 birds. Nests in treetops near or over open water.

male

female

MIGRATION
SUMMER

RUBY-THROATED HUMMINGBIRD
Archilochus colubris

Size: 3-3½" (7.5-9 cm)

Male: Tiny iridescent green bird with black throat patch that reflects bright ruby red in sun.

Female: same as male, but lacking the throat patch

Juvenile: same as female

Nest: cup; female builds; 1-2 broods per year

Eggs: 2; white without markings

Incubation: 12-14 days; female incubates

Fledging: 14-18 days; female feeds young

Migration: complete, to southern states, Mexico and Central America

Food: nectar, insects

Compare: No other bird is as tiny. The Sphinx Moth hovers at flowers like the Hummingbird, but has clear wings and a mouth part that looks like a straw, which coils up when not at a flower. Moves much slower than the Hummingbird and can be approached.

Stan's Notes: The smallest bird in the Dakotas. Able to hover, fly up and down, and is the only bird to fly backward. Does not sing, but will chatter or buzz to communicate. Wings create a humming noise, flapping 50 to 60 times per second or faster during chasing flights. Weighing just 2 to 3 grams, it takes about five average-sized hummingbirds to equal the weight of a single chickadee. Its heart pumps an incredible 1,260 beats per minute, and it breathes 250 times per minute. Constructs a nest with plant material and spider webs, gluing pieces of lichen on the outside of nest for camouflage. Attracted to tubular red flowers.

male

female pg. 161

WOOD DUCK
Aix sponsa

SUMMER

Size: 17-20" (43-50 cm)

Male: A small, highly ornamented dabbling duck with a green head and crest patterned with white and black. A rusty chest, white belly and red eyes.

Female: brown, similar size and shape as male, has bright white eye-ring and a not-so-obvious crest, blue patch on wing often hidden

Juvenile: same as female

Nest: cavity; female lines old woodpecker cavity; 1 brood per year

Eggs: 10-15; creamy white without markings

Incubation: 28-36 days; female incubates

Fledging: 56-68 days; female teaches young to feed

Migration: complete, to southern states

Food: aquatic insects, plants, seeds

Compare: More colorful than male Green-winged Teal (pg. 153). Smaller than the male Shoveler (pg. 243) and lacks the long wide bill.

Stan's Notes: A common duck of quiet, shallow backwater ponds. Nearly extinct around 1900 due to overhunting, but is doing well now. Nests in an old woodpecker hole or uses a nesting box. Often seen flying deep in forest or perched high on tree branches. Female takes flight with loud squealing call and enters nest cavity from full flight. Will lay eggs in a neighboring nest (egg dumping), resulting in some clutches in excess of 20 eggs. Young remain in nest cavity 24 hours after hatching, then jump from up to 30 feet (9 m) to the ground or water to follow their mother, never returning to the nest.

male

female pg. 165

NORTHERN SHOVELER
Anas clypeata

Size: 20" (50 cm)

Male: Medium-sized duck with iridescent green head, rusty sides and white breast. Has an extraordinarily large spoon-shaped bill that is almost always held pointed toward water.

Female: same spoon-shaped bill, brown and black all over and green speculum

Juvenile: same as female

Nest: ground; female builds; 1 brood per year

Eggs: 9-12; olive without markings

Incubation: 22-25 days; female incubates

Fledging: 30-60 days; female leads young to food

Migration: complete, to southern states, Mexico and Central America

Food: aquatic insects, plants

Compare: Similar to the male Mallard (pg. 245), but Shoveler has a large, characteristic spoon-shaped bill. Larger than male Wood Duck (pg. 241) and lacks the Wood Duck's crest.

Stan's Notes: One of several species of shoveler, so called because of the peculiarly shaped bill. The Northern Shoveler is the only species of these ducks in North America. Seen in small flocks of five to ten, swimming low in water with large bills always pointed toward the water, as if they're too heavy to lift. Feeds primarily by filtering tiny plants and insects from the water's surface with bill.

female pg. 181

male

MALLARD
Anas platyrhynchos

Size: 27-28" (69-71 cm)

Male: Large, bulbous green head, white necklace and rust brown or chestnut-colored chest. A combination of gray and white on sides. Yellow bill. Orange legs and feet.

Female: all brown with orange and black bill, small blue and white wing mark (speculum)

Juvenile: same as female, but with a yellow bill

Nest: ground; female builds; 1 brood per year

Eggs: 7-10; greenish to whitish, unmarked

Incubation: 26-30 days; female incubates

Fledging: 42-52 days; female leads young to food

Migration: non-migrator to partial in the Dakotas

Food: seeds, plants, aquatic insects; will come to ground feeders offering corn

Compare: The male Northern Shoveler (pg. 243) has a white chest with rust on sides and a dark spoon-shaped bill. Breeding male Northern Pintail (pg. 179) has very long central tail feathers and a brown head. Male Gadwall (pg. 229) lacks male Mallard's green head.

Stan's Notes: A familiar duck of lakes and ponds, it's considered a type of dabbling duck, tipping forward in shallow water to feed on aquatic plants on the bottom. The name "Mallard" comes from the Latin *masculus*, meaning "male," referring to the habit of males not taking part in raising ducklings. Black central tail feathers of male curl upward. Both the male and female have white tails and white underwings. Will return to place of birth.

male

female pg. 281

AMERICAN REDSTART
Setophaga ruticilla

SUMMER

Size: 5" (13 cm)

Male: Small, striking black bird with contrasting patches of orange on sides, wings and tail. White belly.

Female: olive brown with yellow patches on sides, wings and tail, white belly

Juvenile: same as female, the juvenile male is tinged orange in the first year

Nest: cup; female builds; 1 brood per year

Eggs: 3-5; off-white with brown markings

Incubation: 12 days; female incubates

Fledging: 9 days; female and male feed young

Migration: complete, to Mexico, Central America and South America

Food: insects, seeds, berries rarely

Compare: Male Red-winged Blackbird (pg. 9) and the male Baltimore Oriole (pg. 249) are much larger at roughly 8 inches (20 cm). The only small black and orange bird flitting around tops of trees.

Stan's Notes: A common and widespread breeding warbler in the Dakotas, preferring large unbroken tracts of forest. Appears to be hyperactive when feeding, hovering and darting back and forth to glean insects from leaves. Often droops its wings and fans tail just before launching out to catch an insect. Look for the male's flashing black and orange colors high up in trees.

male

female pg. 291

BALTIMORE ORIOLE
Icterus galbula

MIGRATION
SUMMER

Size:	7-8" (18-20 cm)
Male:	Bright flaming orange bird with black head and black extending down nape of neck onto the back. Black wings with white and orange wing bars. An orange tail with black streaks. Gray bill and dark eyes.
Female:	pale yellow with orange tones, gray brown wings, white wing bars, gray bill, dark eyes
Juvenile:	same as female
Nest:	pendulous; female builds; 1 brood per year
Eggs:	4-5; bluish with brown markings
Incubation:	12-14 days; female incubates
Fledging:	12-14 days; female and male feed young
Migration:	complete, to Mexico, Central America and South America
Food:	insects, fruit, nectar; comes to orange half and nectar feeders
Compare:	The male Orchard Oriole (pg. 251) is much darker orange than the Baltimore's brighter flaming orange color.

Stan's Notes: A fantastic songster, this bird is often heard before seen. Easily attracted to a feeder offering grape jelly, orange halves or sugar water (nectar). Parents bring young to feeders. Sits in tops of trees feeding on caterpillars. Female builds a sock-like nest at the outermost branches of tall trees. Often returns to the same area year after year. Some of the last birds to arrive in spring (March to April) and first to leave in fall (August).

female pg. 293

male

ORCHARD ORIOLE
Icterus spurius

SUMMER

Size: 7-8" (18-20 cm)

Male: Dull orange bird with black head and black extending down the back. A black chin, tail and wings. Single white wing bars. A long, thin black bill with a small gray mark on lower mandible (jaw).

Female: olive green back with dull yellow belly, two white wing bars on dark gray wings

Juvenile: same as female, black bib on first-year male

Nest: pendulous; female builds; 1 brood per year

Eggs: 3-5; pale blue to white, brown markings

Incubation: 11-12 days; female and male incubate

Fledging: 11-14 days; female and male feed young

Migration: complete, central Mexico, Central America and northern South America

Food: insects, fruit; comes to fruit/nectar feeders

Compare: Similar to male Baltimore Oriole (pg. 249), but the male Orchard Oriole has a much darker orange body.

Stan's Notes: Prefers orchards or open woods, hence its common name. Eats insects until wild fruit starts to ripen. One of the last birds to arrive in spring and one of the first to leave in fall. Spends four to five months in the Dakotas. Often migrates with the more abundant Baltimore Oriole. Usually will nest alone, but sometimes nests in small colonies. Parents bring the young to jelly and orange half feeders shortly after fledging. Many people mistakenly think the orioles have left during the summer but, in fact, these birds are concentrating on finding insects to feed their young.

yellow male

female pg. 79

male

HOUSE FINCH
Carpodacus mexicanus

YEAR-ROUND

Size: 5" (13 cm)

Male: An orange red face, breast and rump, with a brown cap. Brown marking behind eyes. Brown wings streaked with white. A white belly with brown streaks.

Female: brown with a heavily streaked white chest

Juvenile: similar to female

Nest: cup, sometimes in cavities; female builds; 2 broods per year

Eggs: 4-5; pale blue, lightly marked

Incubation: 12-14 days; female incubates

Fledging: 15-19 days; female and male feed young

Migration: non-migrator to partial migrator; will move around to find food

Food: seeds, fruit, leaf buds; will visit seed feeders

Compare: Male Purple Finch (pg. 255) is very similar, but male House Finch lacks the red crown. Look for the streaked breast and belly, and brown cap of male House Finch.

Stan's Notes: Very social bird. Visits feeders in small flocks. Likes nesting in hanging flower baskets. Incubating female is fed by the male. Has a loud, cheerful warbling song. House Finches that were originally introduced to Long Island, New York, from the western U.S. in the 1940s have since populated the entire eastern U.S. Now found throughout the country. Suffers from a fatal eye disease that causes eyes to crust over. Rarely, some males are yellow (see inset) instead of red, probably due to poor diet.

female pg. 95

male

PURPLE FINCH
Carpodacus purpureus

Size: 6" (15 cm)

Male: Raspberry red head, cap, breast, back and rump. Brownish wings and tail.

Female: heavily streaked brown and white bird with large white eyebrows

Juvenile: same as female

Nest: cup; female and male build; 1 brood a year

Eggs: 4-5; greenish blue with brown markings

Incubation: 12-13 days; female incubates

Fledging: 13-14 days; female and male feed young

Migration: irruptive; moves around in search of food

Food: seeds, insects, fruit; comes to seed feeders

Compare: Redder than the orange red of male House Finch (pg. 253), with a clear (no streaking) red breast. Male House Finch has a brown crown, compared with male Purple Finch's red cap. Male Red Crossbill (pg. 257) has a unique long crossed bill.

Stan's Notes: Usually only seen in the winter or during migration, when Purple Finches leave their northern homes and move around in search of food. Travels in flocks of up to 50. It is common in non-residential areas (prefers open woods or edges of woodland) and has been replaced in northern cities by House Finches. Feeds primarily on seeds, with seeds of ash trees a very important food source. Will visit seed feeders along with House Finches, making it hard to tell them apart. Has a rich loud song, with a distinctive "tic" note made only in flight. Not a purple color, the Latin species name *purpureus* means "crimson" or other reddish color.

female pg. 287

male

RED CROSSBILL
Loxia curvirostra

Size: 6½" (16 cm)

Male: Sparrow-sized bird, dirty red to orange with bright red crown and rump. Long, pointed, crossed bill. Dark brown wings and a short dark brown tail.

Female: pale yellow chest, light gray throat patch, a crossed bill, dark brown wings and tail

Juvenile: streaked with tinges of yellow, bill gradually crosses about two weeks after fledging

Nest: cup; female builds; 1 brood per year

Eggs: 3-4; bluish white with brown markings

Incubation: 14-18 days; female incubates

Fledging: 16-20 days; female and male feed young

Migration: non-migrator to irruptive; moves around the Dakotas in winter to find food

Food: seeds, leaf buds; comes to seed feeders

Compare: Similar in shape, size and color to the male Purple Finch (pg. 255). Look for the male Red Crossbill's unique bill.

Stan's Notes: The long crossed bill is adapted for extracting seeds from pine and spruce cones, its favorite food. Often dangles upside down like a parrot to reach cones. Also seen on the ground where it eats grit, which helps digest food. Plumage can be highly variable among individuals. Nests in coniferous forests. Though it is a year-round resident in parts of the Dakotas, Red Crossbills from farther north move into North and South Dakota in winter, searching for food, swelling populations. This irruptive behavior makes them more common in some winters and scarce in others.

male

female pg. 123

juvenile

NORTHERN CARDINAL
Cardinalis cardinalis

Size: 8-9" (20-22.5 cm)

Male: All-red bird with a black mask that extends from the face down to the chin and throat. Large red bill and crest.

Female: buff brown with tinges of red on crest and wings, same black mask and red bill

Juvenile: same as female, but with a blackish gray bill

Nest: cup; female builds; 2-3 broods per year

Eggs: 3-4; bluish white with brown markings

Incubation: 12-13 days; female and male incubate

Fledging: 9-10 days; female and male feed young

Migration: non-migrator

Food: seeds, insects, fruit; comes to seed feeders

Compare: The male Red Crossbill (pg. 257) is smaller and has a unique crossed bill. Look for the male Cardinal's black mask, large crest and red bill.

Stan's Notes: A familiar backyard bird. Look for the male feeding female during courtship. Male feeds young of the first brood by himself while female builds second nest. The name comes from the Latin word *cardinalis*, which means "important." Very territorial in spring, it will fight its own reflection in a window. Non-territorial during winter, gathering in small flocks of up to 20 birds. Both the male and female sing and can be heard anytime of year. Listen for its "whata-cheer-cheer-cheer" territorial call in spring.

breeding

winter

HORNED GREBE
Podiceps auritus

MIGRATION
SUMMER

Size: 14" (36 cm)

Male: Breeding plumage (April to August) overall reddish with a black head. Rufous red neck and sides. Dark back. Yellow patch behind red eyes. Small black bill. Winter plumage has a black crown and white face, chin and neck. Red eyes and a white-tipped gray bill.

Female: same as male

Juvenile: similar to winter adult

Nest: floating platform, made of reeds and grass; female and male build; 1 brood per year

Eggs: 3-5; light blue with light markings

Incubation: 22-25 days; female and male incubate

Fledging: 20-40 days; male and female teach young what to eat

Migration: complete, to the Pacific, Gulf and Atlantic coasts

Food: fish, aquatic insects

Compare: Eared Grebe (pg. 17) is slightly smaller and has a black during breeding season.

Stan's Notes: A grebe of pothole lakes and ponds. Will often dive underwater to avoid danger, swimming up to 500 feet (150 m) before resurfacing. In an elaborate courtship display similar to the Western Grebe, male and female rise up side by side out of water and "rush" across the surface. Will shake heads and present weeds to each other as presents. Usually in pairs, building a platform nest in shallow water, continuing construction while female lays eggs. Young hatch several days apart. Chicks ride on backs of parents.

in flight

FORSTER'S TERN
Sterna forsteri

Size: 14-15" (36-38 cm)

Male: White and gray tern with a jet black crown and an orange bill with a black tip. Leading edge of wings is gray, trailing edge is white. Characteristic forked tail is long and white. Winter plumage lacks black crown and bill becomes nearly entirely black.

Female: same as male

Juvenile: similar to adult, lacks the black crown

Nest: floating platform; female and male build; 1 brood per year

Eggs: 3-5; tan to white with brown markings

Incubation: 23-24 days; female and male incubate

Fledging: 24-26 days; male and female feed young

Migration: complete, to southern coastal states, Mexico and Central America

Food: small fish, aquatic insects

Compare: Larger than the Black Tern (pg. 11), which has a black head and chest during breeding season. Look for the black crown and black-tipped orange bill of the breeding Forster's.

Stan's Notes: Usually is seen in small colonies summering in the eastern Dakotas. Catches fish by diving into water headfirst. Will catch insects in flight. Builds a platform nest on floating vegetation. Nests in shallow-water marshes. Was named after Johann Reinhold Forster, a German naturalist who traveled around the world with Captain Cook in 1772.

winter

juvenile

breeding

MIGRATION
SUMMER
WINTER

RING-BILLED GULL
Larus delawarensis

Size: 19" (48 cm); up to 4-foot wingspan

Male: A white bird with gray wings, black wing tips spotted with white, and a white tail, as seen in flight. Yellow bill with a black ring near tip. Yellowish legs and feet. Winter or non-breeding adult has a speckled brown back of head and nape of neck.

Female: same as male

Juvenile: mostly gray version of winter adult, has dark band at end of tail

Nest: ground; the female and male build; 1 brood per year

Eggs: 2-4; off-white with brown markings

Incubation: 20-21 days; female and male incubate

Fledging: 20-40 days; female and male feed young

Migration: complete, southern states, Mexico; winters in southeastern South Dakota

Food: insects, fish; scavenges for food

Compare: A large white and gray gull. Look for a black ring near the tip of a yellow bill, and yellow legs and feet.

Stan's Notes: A common gull of garbage dumps and parking lots. It's expanding its range and remains farther north longer in winter due to successful scavenging in cities. A three-year gull, acquiring a new, different plumage in each of the first three autumns. Attains ring on bill after its first winter. Doesn't attain adult plumage until the third year. Defends a small area around nest, usually a few feet.

white
morph

blue morph

juvenile

in flight

MIGRATION

SNOW GOOSE
Chen caerulescens

Size: 25-38" (63-96 cm)

Male: A mostly white goose with varying patches of black and brown. Black wing tips. Pink bill and legs. Some birds are grayish with a white head.

Female: same as male

Juvenile: overall dull gray with a dark bill

Nest: ground; female builds; 1 brood per year

Eggs: 3-5; white without markings

Incubation: 23-25 days; female incubates

Fledging: 45-49 days; female and male teach young to feed

Migration: complete, to southern states, New Mexico, California and Mexico

Food: aquatic insects and plants

Compare: Smaller than the Canada Goose (pg. 233), lacking a black neck and white chin strap. Tundra and Trumpeter Swans (pp. 271 and 273, respectively) lack the black wing tips. Pelican (pg. 275) has an enormous bill.

Stan's Notes: Two color morphs. The more common white morph is pure white with black wing tips. Gray morph is often called blue, with a white head, gray chest and back, and pink bill and legs. Has a thick serrated bill for pulling up plants. Breeds in large colonies on the tundra of northern Canada. Females don't breed until they are 2 to 3 years old. Older females produce more eggs and are more successful than the younger females. Seen by the tens of thousands during migration. Often associated with Sandhill Cranes.

GREAT EGRET
Ardea alba

Size: 38" (96 cm)

Male: Tall, thin, elegant all-white bird with long, pointed yellow bill. Black stilt-like legs and black feet.

Female: same as male

Juvenile: same as adult

Nest: platform; male and female build; 1 brood per year

Eggs: 2-3; light blue without markings

Incubation: 23-26 days; female and male incubate

Fledging: 43-49 days; female and male feed young

Migration: complete, to southern states, Mexico and Central America

Food: fish, aquatic insects, frogs, crayfish

Compare: The Great Blue Heron (pg. 237) is larger in size, but has a similar shape.

Stan's Notes: A tall and stately bird, the Great Egret slowly stalks shallow wetlands looking for small fish to spear with its long sharp bill. Nests in colonies of up to 100 birds. Now protected, they were hunted to near extinction in the 1800s and early 1900s for their long white plumage. The name "Egret" came from the French word *aigrette*, which means "ornamental tufts of plumes." The plumes grow near the tail during breeding season.

in flight

MIGRATION

TUNDRA SWAN
Cygnus columbianus

Size: 50-54" (127-137 cm); up to 5½-ft. wingspan

Male: Large all-white swan with all-black bill, legs and feet. Has a small yellow mark in front of each eye.

Female: same as male

Juvenile: same size as adult, gray plumage, pinkish gray bill

Nest: ground; the female and male build; 1 brood per year

Eggs: 4-5; creamy white without markings

Incubation: 35-40 days; female and male incubate

Fledging: 60-70 days; female and male feed young

Migration: complete, to the East coast

Food: plants, aquatic insects

Compare: The Trumpeter Swan (pg. 273) is larger and lacks yellow marks on its face. Snow Goose (pg. 267) is much smaller and has black wing tips. Look for the black bill and legs.

Stan's Notes: Nests on the tundra of northern Canada and Alaska, hence its common name. Usually seen only during fall migration; returns north via a different route. Migrates diagonally across North America to reach wintering grounds along the East coast. Gathers in large numbers in some lakes and rivers to rest, usually staying until the water freezes before continuing to migrate. Flies in large V-shaped wedges. Often seen in large family groups consisting of 20 or more individuals. Young are easy to distinguish by their gray plumage and pinkish bills. Gives a high-pitched, whistle-like call.

in flight

juvenile

TRUMPETER SWAN
Cygnus buccinator

Size: 60" (152 cm); up to 6½-foot wingspan

Male: Large all-white swan with all-black bill, legs and feet.

Female: same as male

Juvenile: same size as adult, gray plumage, pinkish gray bill

Nest: ground; the female and male build; 1 brood per year

Eggs: 4-6; creamy white without markings

Incubation: 33-37 days; female incubates

Fledging: 100-120 days; female and male feed young

Migration: partial to complete, to southern states; some will stay in South Dakota during winter on open water

Food: aquatic plants, insects

Compare: Very similar to the Tundra Swan (pg. 271), which is smaller and has a small yellow mark in front of each eye. Twice the average size of the Snow Goose (pg. 267) and lacks the Snow Goose's black wing tips.

Stan's Notes: Once eliminated from North and South Dakota due to market hunting, but has been reintroduced with great success. Often seen with large colored neck or wing tags, which identify reintroduced individuals. Holds neck with a slight bend or kink at the base. Pairs defend large territories and construct large mound nests at edges of water. Many flock to open water on the Missouri River in winter. Common name comes from its trumpet-like call.

chick-feeding
adult

AMERICAN WHITE PELICAN
Pelecanus erythrorhynchos

Size: 62" (158 cm); up to 9-foot wingspan

Male: A large white bird with black wing tips that extend partially down the trailing edge of wings. A white or pale yellow crown. Bright yellow bill, legs and feet. Breeding adult has a bright orange bill and legs. An adult that is feeding chicks (chick-feeding adult) has a gray-black crown.

Female: same as male

Juvenile: duller white with brownish head and neck

Nest: ground, a scraped-out depression rimmed with dirt; female and male build; 1 brood per year

Eggs: 1-3; white without markings

Incubation: 29-36 days; male and female incubate

Fledging: 60-70 days; female and male feed young

Migration: complete, Central and South America

Food: fish

Compare: Snow Goose (pg. 267) is much smaller and lacks the Pelican's enormous bill.

Stan's Notes: Frequently seen in large groups on the larger lakes and reservoirs of the Dakotas during migration and summer. They feed by simultaneously dipping their bills in water to scoop up fish. They don't dive in water to catch fish, like coastal Brown Pelicans. Bills and legs of breeding adults turn deep orange. Breeding adults usually also grow a flat fibrous plate in the middle of the upper mandible. This plate drops off after eggs have hatched. They fly in a large V, often gliding with long wings, then all flapping together.

male

winter male

female

AMERICAN GOLDFINCH
Carduelis tristis

Size: 5" (13 cm)

Male: A perky yellow bird with a black patch on forehead. Black tail with conspicuous white rump. Black wings with white wing bars. No marking on the chest. Dramatic change in color during winter, similar to female.

Female: dull olive yellow without a black forehead, with brown wings and a white rump

Juvenile: same as female

Nest: cup; female builds; 1 brood per year

Eggs: 4-6; pale blue without markings

Incubation: 10-12 days; female incubates

Fledging: 11-17 days; female and male feed young

Migration: partial migrator to non-migrator; flocks of up to 20 move around North America

Food: seeds, insects; will come to seed feeders

Compare: Male Yellow Warbler (pg. 283) is all yellow with orange streaking on chest. Pine Siskin (pg. 77) has a streaked chest and belly, with yellow wing bars. The female House Finch (pg. 79) and female Purple Finch (pg. 95) both have heavily streaked chests.

Stan's Notes: Most often found in open fields, scrubby areas and woodlands. Often called Wild Canary. A feeder bird that enjoys Nyjer Thistle. Late summer nesting, uses the silky down from wild thistle for nest. Appears roller-coaster-like in flight. Listen for it to twitter during flight. Almost always in small flocks. Moves only far enough south to find food.

SUMMER

COMMON YELLOWTHROAT
Geothlypis trichas

Size: 5" (13 cm)

Male: Olive brown bird with bright yellow throat and breast, a white belly and a distinctive black mask outlined in white. A long, thin, pointed black bill.

Female: same as male, but lacking the black mask

Juvenile: same as female

Nest: cup; female builds; 2 broods per year

Eggs: 3-5; white with brown markings

Incubation: 11-12 days; female incubates

Fledging: 10-11 days; female and male feed young

Migration: complete, to southern states, Mexico and Central America

Food: insects

Compare: Found in a similar habitat as the American Goldfinch (pg. 277), but lacks the male's black forehead and wings. The male Yellow Warbler (pg. 283) has fine orange streaks on chest and lacks the black mask. Yellow-rumped Warbler (pg. 199) has only spots of yellow, compared with the Yellowthroat's yellow breast.

Stan's Notes: A common warbler of open fields and marshes. Has a cheerful, well-known song, "witchity-witchity-witchity-witchity." The male performs a curious courtship display, bouncing in and out of tall grass while uttering an unusual song. The young remain dependent upon the parents longer than most warblers. A frequent cowbird host.

male pg. 247

female

AMERICAN REDSTART
Setophaga ruticilla

Size: 5" (13 cm)

Female: Olive brown with yellow patches on sides, wings and tail. White belly.

Male: small, striking black bird with contrasting patches of orange on sides, wings and tail, white belly

Juvenile: same as female, the juvenile male is tinged orange in the first year

Nest: cup; female builds; 1 brood per year

Eggs: 3-5; off-white with brown markings

Incubation: 12 days; female incubates

Fledging: 9 days; female and male feed young

Migration: complete, to Mexico, Central America and South America

Food: insects, seeds, berries rarely

Compare: Similar to female Yellow-rumped Warbler (pg. 199), but lacking the Warbler's yellow patch on rump.

Stan's Notes: A common and widespread breeding warbler in the Dakotas, preferring large unbroken tracts of forest. Appears to be hyperactive when feeding, hovering and darting back and forth to glean insects from leaves. Often droops its wings and fans tail just before launching out to catch an insect. Look for the male's flashing black and orange colors high up in trees.

YELLOW WARBLER
Dendroica petechia

Size: 5" (13 cm)

Male: Yellow warbler with orange streaks on the chest and belly. Long, pointed dark bill.

Female: same as male, but lacking orange streaking

Juvenile: similar to female, only much duller

Nest: cup; female builds; 1 brood per year

Eggs: 4-5; white with brown markings

Incubation: 11-12 days; female incubates

Fledging: 10-12 days; female and male feed young

Migration: complete, to southern states, Mexico, and Central and South America

Food: insects

Compare: Yellow-rumped Warbler (pg. 199) has only spots of yellow, compared with the orange streaking on chest of male Yellow Warbler. Male American Goldfinch (pg. 277) has black wings and forehead. Female Warbler is similar to the female American Goldfinch (pg. 277), but lacks the white wing bars.

Stan's Notes: A scattered but widespread breeding warbler in the Dakotas. More common in eastern areas, it is seen in gardens and shrubby areas close to water. A prolific insect eater, gleaning small caterpillars and other insects from tree leaves. The male is usually seen higher up in trees than the female. Female is less conspicuous. Starts to migrate in August. Returns in April. Males arrive a week or two before the females to claim territories. Migrates at night in mixed flocks of warblers. Rests and feeds days.

283

male

female

SUMMER

DICKCISSEL
Spiza americana

Size: 6" (15 cm)

Male: A small thick-billed bird with yellow chest, belly and eyebrows, and chestnut wings. A distinctive black bib under a white chin.

Female: same as male, but lacking the black bib

Juvenile: similar to female, only duller overall

Nest: cup, made of plant stems, grass and leaves; female builds; 1 brood per year

Eggs: 4-6; pale blue without markings

Incubation: 12-13 days; female incubates

Fledging: 9-11 days; female feeds young

Migration: complete, to Mexico, Central America and South America

Food: insects, seeds

Compare: Western Meadowlark (pg. 297) is larger and has a prominent black V-shaped necklace, compared with the Dickcissel's black bib.

Stan's Notes: Originally a bird of the prairie, now found in alfalfa fields, abandoned fields and meadows due to the loss of native prairie habitat. Prefers habitat that is sparsely vegetative. Doesn't do well in thick, dense vegetation. The males arrive at breeding sites a couple weeks before the females and begin to sing from prominent perches. Often seen singing from a fence post because it's the tallest object around. Nest is bulky, only a couple feet above ground and usually well concealed. Common name comes from an imitation of its song.

female

male pg. 257

RED CROSSBILL
Loxia curvirostra

Size: 6½" (16 cm)

Female: A pale yellow-gray sparrow-sized bird with a pale yellow chest and light gray patch on the throat. Long, pointed, crossed bill. Dark brown wings and a short dark brown tail.

Male: dirty red to orange with a bright red crown and rump, a crossed bill, dark brown wings and a short dark brown tail

Juvenile: streaked with tinges of yellow, bill gradually crosses about two weeks after fledging

Nest: cup; female builds; 1 brood per year

Eggs: 3-4; bluish white with brown markings

Incubation: 14-18 days; female incubates

Fledging: 16-20 days; female and male feed young

Migration: non-migrator to irruptive; moves around the Dakotas in winter to find food

Food: seeds, leaf buds; comes to seed feeders

Compare: Similar in shape and size to female Purple Finch (pg. 95). Look for the female Red Crossbill's unique bill.

Stan's Notes: The long crossed bill is adapted for extracting seeds from pine and spruce cones, its favorite food. Often dangles upside down like a parrot to reach cones. Also seen on the ground where it eats grit, which helps digest food. Plumage can be highly variable among individuals. Nests in coniferous forests. Red Crossbills from farther north migrate into the Dakotas during winter, searching for food, swelling populations. This irruptive behavior makes them more common in some winters and scarce in others.

non-breeding male

breeding male

female

MIGRATION
SUMMER

WESTERN TANAGER
Piranga ludoviciana

Size: 7¼" (18.5 cm)

Male: A canary yellow bird with a red head. Black back, tail, wings. One white and one yellow wing bar. Non-breeding lacks the red head.

Female: duller than male, lacking the red head

Juvenile: similar to female

Nest: cup; female builds; 1 brood per year

Eggs: 3-5; light blue with brown markings

Incubation: 11-13 days; female incubates

Fledging: 13-15 days; female and male feed young

Migration: complete, to Mexico and Central America

Food: insects, fruit

Compare: Male American Goldfinch (pg. 277) has a black forehead and lacks the breeding male Tanager's red head. Unique combination of colors makes the male hard to misidentify. Female Orchard Oriole (pg. 293) lacks the female Tanager's single yellow wing bars.

Stan's Notes: Seen during migration in parts of the Dakotas, it summers in the Black Hills of South Dakota. The male is stunning in breeding plumage. Feeds mainly on insects such as bees, wasps, grasshoppers and cicadas. Feeds to a lesser degree on fruit. Male feeds female as she incubates. Nests in a horizontal fork of a conifer, well away from the main trunk; from 20 to 40 feet (6 to 12 m) above ground. The farthest nesting tanager species, reaching far up into Canada's Northwest Territories. An early fall migrant, often migrating in late July (when non-breeding males lack red-colored heads). Can be seen in just about any habitat during migration.

male pg. 249

female

MIGRATION
SUMMER

BALTIMORE ORIOLE
Icterus galbula

Size: 7-8" (18-20 cm)

Female: A pale yellow bird with orange tones, gray brown wings, white wing bars, a gray bill and dark eyes.

Male: bright flaming orange bird with black head and black extending down nape of neck onto the back, black wings with white and orange wing bars, an orange tail with black streaks, gray bill and dark eyes

Juvenile: same as female

Nest: pendulous; female builds; 1 brood per year

Eggs: 4-5; bluish with brown markings

Incubation: 12-14 days; female incubates

Fledging: 12-14 days; female and male feed young

Migration: complete, to Mexico, Central America and South America

Food: insects, fruit, nectar; comes to orange half and nectar feeders

Compare: Very similar to the female Orchard Oriole (pg. 293), which lacks orange tones and has less pronounced wing bars.

Stan's Notes: A fantastic songster, this bird is often heard before seen. Easily attracted to a feeder offering grape jelly, orange halves or sugar water (nectar). Parents bring young to feeders. Sits in tops of trees feeding on caterpillars. Female builds a sock-like nest at the outermost branches of tall trees. Often returns to the same area year after year. Some of the last birds to arrive in spring (March to April) and first to leave in fall (August).

male pg. 251

female

ORCHARD ORIOLE
Icterus spurius

SUMMER

Size: 7-8" (18-20 cm)

Female: An olive green bird with a dull yellow belly. Two white wing bars on dark gray wings. Long, thin black bill with a small gray mark on lower mandible (jaw).

Male: dull orange with a black head, chin, upper back, wings and tail, single white wing bars

Juvenile: same as female, black bib on first-year male

Nest: pendulous; female builds; 1 brood per year

Eggs: 3-5; pale blue to white, brown markings

Incubation: 11-12 days; female and male incubate

Fledging: 11-14 days; female and male feed young

Migration: complete, central Mexico, Central America and northern South America

Food: insects, fruit; comes to fruit/nectar feeders

Compare: Female Baltimore Oriole (pg. 291) is similar, but has orange tones and more pronounced wing bars.

Stan's Notes: Prefers orchards or open woods, hence its common name. Eats insects until wild fruit starts to ripen. One of the last birds to arrive in spring and one of the first to leave in fall. Spends four to five months in the Dakotas. Often migrates with the more abundant Baltimore Oriole. Usually nests alone; sometimes nests in small colonies. Parents bring young to jelly and orange half feeders just after fledging. Many think the orioles have left in summer, but the birds are concentrating on finding insects to feed their young.

SUMMER

WESTERN KINGBIRD
Tyrannus verticalis

Size: 9" (22.5 cm)

Male: Bright yellow belly and yellow under wings. Gray head and chest, often with white chin. Wings and tail are dark gray to nearly black with white outer edges on tail.

Female: same as male

Juvenile: similar to adult, less yellow and more gray

Nest: cup; female and male build; 1 brood a year

Eggs: 3-4; white with brown markings

Incubation: 18-20 days; female incubates

Fledging: 16-18 days; female and male feed young

Migration: complete, to Central America

Food: insects, berries

Compare: The Eastern Kingbird (pg. 207) lacks any yellow of the Western Kingbird. Western Meadowlark (pg. 297) shares the Western Kingbird's yellow belly, but has a distinctive black V-shaped necklace.

Stan's Notes: A bird of open country, often seen sitting on top of the same shrub or fence post. Hunts by watching for insects, such as bees, grasshoppers and crickets, then flying out to catch them and returning to its perch. Parents teach young how to hunt, often bringing wounded insects back to the nest for the young to chase. Returns in April, nest building in May. Often builds nest in the fork of a small single trunk tree. More common in the western and central Dakotas, where it nests in trees around homesteads and farms.

WESTERN MEADOWLARK
Sturnella neglecta

YEAR-ROUND
SUMMER

Size: 9" (22.5 cm)

Male: Heavy-bodied bird with a short tail. Brown back, yellow chest and prominent black V-shaped necklace. White outer tail feathers.

Female: same as male

Juvenile: same as adult

Nest: cup, on the ground in dense cover; female builds; 1-2 broods per year

Eggs: 3-5; white with brown markings

Incubation: 13-15 days; female incubates

Fledging: 11-13 days; female and male feed young

Migration: partial migrator to non-migrator

Food: insects, seeds

Compare: Western Kingbird (pg. 295) shares a yellow belly, but lacks the Meadowlark's distinctive black V-shaped necklace.

Stan's Notes: This bird is most common in open country. Named "Meadowlark" because it's a bird of meadows and sings like larks of Europe. Best known for its wonderful song. Not a member of the lark family, it belongs to the blackbird family. Related to blackbirds such as grackles and orioles. Like other blackbird family members, it catches prey by poking its long thin bill into places such as holes in the ground or in tufts of grass, where bugs are hiding. Opening its mouth to create space, the bird extracts insects. Often perches on fence posts. Quickly dives into tall grass if approached. Seen in the western two-thirds of the Dakotas, while Eastern Meadowlarks occur in eastern areas (map reflects their combined range). Nearly identical in appearance, but they sing distinctly different songs.

Helpful Resources:

Birder's Bug Book, The. Waldbauer, Gilbert. Cambridge: Harvard University Press, 1998.

Birder's Dictionary. Cox, Randall T. Helena, MT: Falcon Press Publishing, 1996.

Birder's Handbook, The. Ehrlich, Paul R., David S. Dobkin and Darryl Wheye. New York: Simon and Schuster, 1988.

Birds Do It, Too: The Amazing Sex Life of Birds. Harrison, Kit and George H. Harrison. Minocqua, WI: Willow Creek Press, 1997.

Birds of Forest, Yard, and Thicket. Eastman, John. Mechanicsburg, PA: Stackpole Books, 1997.

Birds of North America. Kaufman, Kenn. New York: Houghton Mifflin, 2000.

Cry of the Sandhill Crane, The. Grooms, Steve. Minocqua, WI: NorthWord Press, 1992.

Dictionary of American Bird Names, The. Choate, Ernest A. Boston: Harvard Common Press, 1985.

Everything You Never Learned About Birds. Rupp, Rebecca. Pownal, VT: Storey Publishing, 1997.

Field Guide to the Birds, A: A Completely New Guide to All the Birds of Eastern and Central North America. Peterson, Roger Tory and Virginia Marie Peterson. Boston: Houghton Mifflin, 1998.

Field Guide to the Birds of North America: Third Edition. Washington, DC: National Geographic Society, 1999.

Field Guide to Warblers of North America, A. Dunn, Jon and Kimball Garrett. Boston: Houghton Mifflin, 1997.

Field Guide to Western Birds, A. Peterson, Roger Tory. Boston: Houghton Mifflin, 1998.

Folklore of Birds. Martin, Laura C. Old Saybrook, CT: Globe Pequot Press, 1996.

Guide to Bird Behavior, A: Vol I, II, III. Stokes, Donald and Lillian Stokes. Boston: Little, Brown and Company, 1989.

How Birds Migrate. Kerlinger, Paul. Mechanicsburg, PA: Stackpole Books, 1995.

Lives of Birds, The: Birds of the World and Their Behavior. Short, Lester L. Collingdale, PA: DIANE Publishing, 2000.

Lives of North American Birds. Kaufman, Kenn. Boston: Houghton Mifflin, 1996.

Living on the Wind. Weidensaul, Scott. New York: North Point Press, 2000.

National Audubon Society: North American Birdfeeder Handbook. Burton, Robert. New York: Dorling Kindersley Publishing, 1995.

National Audubon Society: The Sibley Guide to Bird Life and Behavior. Edited by David Allen Sibley, Chris Elphick and John B. Dunning, Jr. New York: Alfred A. Knopf, 2001.

National Audubon Society: The Sibley Guide to Birds. Sibley, David Allen. New York: Alfred A. Knopf, 2000.

Photographic Guide to North American Raptors, A. Wheeler, Brian K. and William S. Clark. New York: Academic Press, 1999.

Secret Lives of Birds, The. Gingras, Pierre. Toronto: Key Porter Books, 1997.

Secrets of the Nest. Dunning, Joan. Boston: Houghton Mifflin, 1994.

Sparrows and Buntings. Byers, Clive, Jon Curson and Urban Olsson. New York: Houghton Mifflin, 1995.

Stokes Bluebird Book: The Complete Guide to Attracting Bluebirds. Stokes, Donald and Lillian Stokes. Boston: Little, Brown and Company, 1991.

Stokes Field Guide to Birds: Eastern Region. Stokes, Donald and Lillian Stokes. Boston: Little, Brown and Company, 1996.

Stokes Field Guide to Birds: Western Region. Stokes, Donald and Lillian Stokes. Boston: Little, Brown and Company, 1996.

Stokes Purple Martin Book. Stokes, Donald and Lillian Stokes. Boston: Little, Brown and Company, 1997.

For reporting unusual bird sightings or to hear a recording of where birds have been seen, contact:

North Dakota Statewide	South Dakota Statewide	Western
701-250-4481	605-773-6460	605-584-4141

WEB PAGES:

The Internet is a valuable place to learn about birds. Following are web sites to assist you in your pursuit of birds. You may find birding on the Net a fun way to learn more about birds or spend a long winter night.

SITE	ADDRESS
North Dakota Birding Society	www.datatools.org/ndbirdingsociety
South Dakota Ornithologists' Union	www.homepages.dsu.edu/palmerj/SDOU/SDOU.html
American Birding Association	www.americanbirding.org
Cornell Lab of Ornithology	www.birds.cornell.edu
Author Stan Tekiela's home page	www.naturesmart.com

Use the boxes to check the birds you've seen.

☐ Avocet, American 43

☐ Bittern, American.............183

☐ Blackbird,
Red-winged 9, 125

☐ Blackbird,
Yellow-headed 13, 133

☐ Bluebird, Eastern 61

☐ Bluebird, Mountain 63

☐ Bunting, Lark.............31, 101

☐ Bunting, Lazuli.............55, 85

☐ Bunting, Snow 33

☐ Cardinal, Northern ..123, 259

☐ Catbird, Gray 209

☐ Chickadee, Black-capped..195

☐ Chicken, Greater Prairie- ..159

☐ Coot, American 19

☐ Cormorant,
Double-crested 25

☐ Cowbird,
Brown-headed 3, 119

☐ Crane, Sandhill 235

☐ Crossbill, Red............257, 287

☐ Crow, American 21

☐ Dickcissel 285

☐ Dove, Mourning...............145

☐ Duck, Wood 161, 241

☐ Eagle, Bald 53

☐ Egret, Great 269

☐ Finch, House 79, 253

☐ Finch, Purple 95, 255

☐ Flicker, Northern 143

☐ Flycatcher, Great Crested..205

☐ Gadwall 167, 229

☐ Goldeneye, Common..45, 163

☐ Goldfinch, American 277

☐ Goose, Canada 233

☐ Goose,
Greater White-fronted 185

☐ Goose, Snow 267

☐ Grackle, Common 15

☐ Grebe, Eared 17

☐ Grebe, Horned 261

☐ Grebe, Pied-billed 149

☐ Grebe, Western 51

☐ Grosbeak,
Rose-breasted..............35, 111

☐ Gull, Franklin's 223

☐ Gull, Ring-billed 265

☐ Harrier, Northern......177, 231

☐ Hawk, Cooper's 227

☐ Hawk, Ferruginous 175

☐ Hawk, Red-tailed 171

☐ Hawk, Sharp-shinned 219

☐ Hawk, Swainson's 169

☐ Heron,
Black-crowned Night- 49

☐ Heron, Great Blue 237

☐ Hummingbird,

Ruby-throated 239
☐ Jay, Blue 67
☐ Junco, Dark-eyed........83, 201
☐ Kestrel, American..............141
☐ Killdeer.............................137
☐ Kingbird, Eastern 207
☐ Kingbird, Western 295
☐ Kingfisher, Belted 69
☐ Kinglet, Ruby-crowned 191
☐ Lark, Horned 113
☐ Longspur,
Chestnut-collared................97
☐ Longspur, Lapland 99
☐ Magpie, Black-billed 47
☐ Mallard.....................181, 245
☐ Martin, Purple 65
☐ Meadowlark, Western 297
☐ Nighthawk, Common 129
☐ Night-Heron,
Black-crowned 49
☐ Nuthatch, Red-breasted 193
☐ Nuthatch,
White-breasted..................197
☐ Oriole, Baltimore 249, 291
☐ Oriole, Orchard 251, 293
☐ Owl, Burrowing 131
☐ Owl, Eastern Screech- 213
☐ Owl, Great Horned 173
☐ Pelican, American White ..275
☐ Phalarope, Wilson's 215

☐ Pheasant, Ring-necked......187
☐ Phoebe, Eastern 203
☐ Pigeon, Rock 221
☐ Pintail, Northern 179
☐ Prairie-Chicken, Greater ..159
☐ Redpoll, Common 73
☐ Redstart, American ..247, 281
☐ Robin, American 217
☐ Sandpiper, Spotted...........121
☐ Sandpiper, Upland...........147
☐ Scaup, Lesser 41, 157
☐ Screech-Owl, Eastern........213
☐ Shoveler, Northern ..165, 243
☐ Shrike, Loggerhead 209
☐ Siskin, Pine 77
☐ Sparrow, American Tree 91
☐ Sparrow, Chipping.............75
☐ Sparrow, Harris's...............117
☐ Sparrow, House 93
☐ Sparrow, Lark...................103
☐ Sparrow, Song 89
☐ Sparrow, White-crowned ..107
☐ Sparrow, White-throated ..105
☐ Starling, European 5
☐ Swallow, Barn.....................59
☐ Swallow, Cliff 87
☐ Swallow, Tree 57
☐ Swan, Trumpeter...............273
☐ Swan, Tundra....................271
☐ Swift, Chimney 71

☐ Tanager, Western 289
☐ Teal, Blue-winged..............155
☐ Teal, Green-winged 153
☐ Tern, Black 11
☐ Tern, Forster's....................263
☐ Thrasher, Brown................139
☐ Thrush, Swainson's 109
☐ Towhee, Spotted 7, 127
☐ Turkey, Wild.....................189
☐ Vulture, Turkey 23
☐ Warbler, Black-and-white ..27
☐ Warbler, Yellow 283
☐ Warbler, Yellow-rumped ..199
☐ Waxwing, Bohemian 114
☐ Waxwing, Cedar 115
☐ Willet 151, 225
☐ Woodpecker, Downy 29
☐ Woodpecker, Hairy 37
☐ Woodpecker, Red-headed ..39
☐ Wren, House 81
☐ Yellowlegs, Lesser..............135
☐ Yellowthroat, Common 279

ABOUT THE AUTHOR:

Stan Tekiela is a naturalist, author and wildlife photographer with a Bachelor of Science degree in Natural History from the University of Minnesota. He has been a professional naturalist for more than 20 years and is a member of the Minnesota Naturalist Association, Minnesota Ornithologist Union, Outdoor Writers Association of America, North American Nature Photography Association and Canon Professional Services. Stan actively studies and photographs birds throughout the United States. He has received various national and regional awards for outdoor education and writing. A columnist and radio personality, his syndicated column appears in over 20 cities and he can be heard on a number of radio stations. Stan resides in Victoria, Minnesota, with wife Katherine and daughter Abigail. He can be contacted via his web page at www.naturesmart.com.

Stan authors field guides for other states including guides for birds, birds of prey, mammals, reptiles and amphibians, trees and wildflowers.